The Stranger's Guide through Cheltenham; containing an account of its mineral waters ... Also, notices of the principal objects of curiosity in the surrounding country. [The preface signed: H. D., i.e. H. Davies. With plates and maps.]

Henry Davies

The Stranger's Guide through Cheltenham; containing an account of its mineral waters ... Also, notices of the principal objects of curiosity in the surrounding country. [The preface signed: H. D., i.e. H. Davies. With plates and maps.]

Davies, Henry
British Library, Historical Print Editions
British Library
1843
vi. 220 p. ; 8°.
797.e.17.

The BiblioLife Network

This project was made possible in part by the BiblioLife Network (BLN), a project aimed at addressing some of the huge challenges facing book preservationists around the world. The BLN includes libraries, library networks, archives, subject matter experts, online communities and library service providers. We believe every book ever published should be available as a high-quality print reproduction; printed on- demand anywhere in the world. This insures the ongoing accessibility of the content and helps generate sustainable revenue for the libraries and organizations that work to preserve these important materials.

The following book is in the "public domain" and represents an authentic reproduction of the text as printed by the original publisher. While we have attempted to accurately maintain the integrity of the original work, there are sometimes problems with the original book or micro-film from which the books were digitized. This can result in minor errors in reproduction. Possible imperfections include missing and blurred pages, poor pictures, markings and other reproduction issues beyond our control. Because this work is culturally important, we have made it available as part of our commitment to protecting, preserving, and promoting the world's literature.

GUIDE TO FOLD-OUTS, MAPS and OVERSIZED IMAGES

In an online database, page images do not need to conform to the size restrictions found in a printed book. When converting these images back into a printed bound book, the page sizes are standardized in ways that maintain the detail of the original. For large images, such as fold-out maps, the original page image is split into two or more pages.

Guidelines used to determine the split of oversize pages:

• Some images are split vertically; large images require vertical and horizontal splits.
• For horizontal splits, the content is split left to right.
• For vertical splits, the content is split from top to bottom.
• For both vertical and horizontal splits, the image is processed from top left to bottom right.

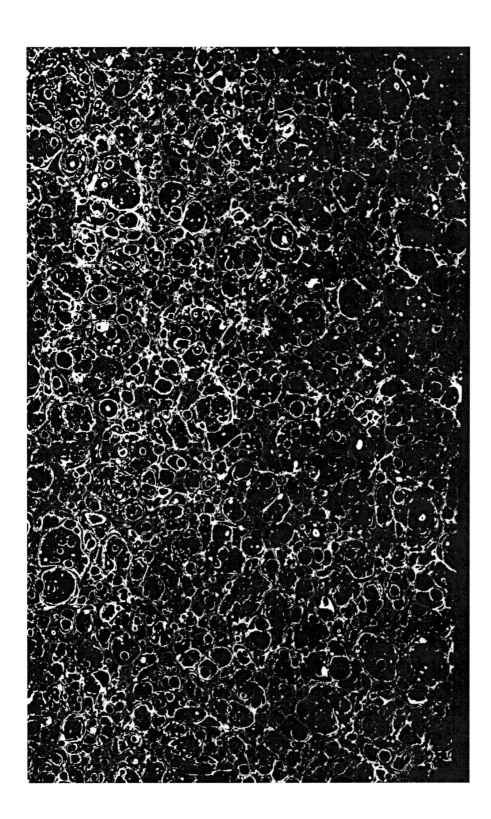

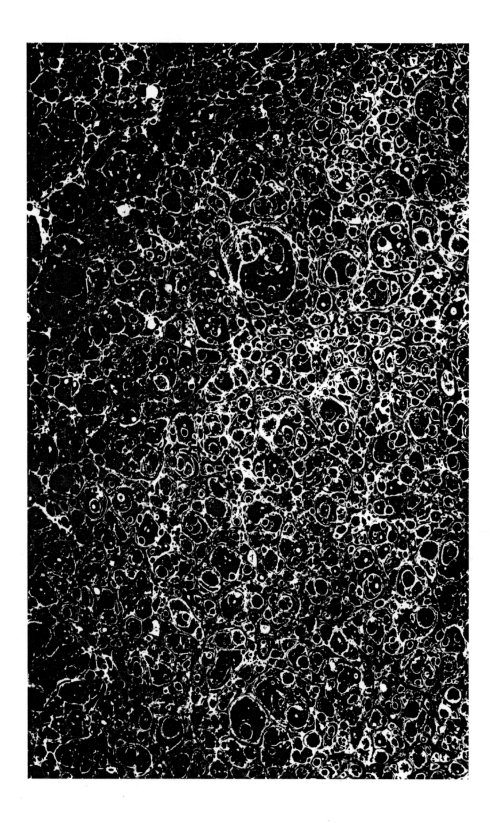

A VIEW

OF

CHELTENHAM,

IN ITS

PAST AND PRESENT STATE,

BEING THE

FOURTH EDITION

OF

The Stranger's Guide.

H. DAVIES, MONTPELLIER LIBRARY, CHELTENHAM.

A VIEW

OF

CHELTENHAM,

IN ITS

PAST AND PRESENT STATE,

BEING THE

FOURTH EDITION

OF

THE STRANGER'S GUIDE;

ENLARGED BY THE INTRODUCTION OF MUCH ADDITIONAL INFORMATION;

AND

ILLUSTRATED WITH NUMEROUS

Lithographs, Maps, and Wood Engravings.

———

BY

HENRY DAVIES.

———

CHELTENHAM:

H. DAVIES, MONTPELLIER LIBRARY.

G. A. WILLIAMS, J. LEE, J. LOVESY, J. ALDER;

AND

LONGMAN & Co., LONDON.

PREFACE.

THE very favourable reception which the former
Editions of the STRANGER'S GUIDE THROUGH CHEL-
TENHAM experienced, has encouraged its Author to
undertake the enlarged and Pictorial Edition now
presented to the public, in order more fully to exhibit "The Town in its Past and Present State,"
than appeared necessary to be done, or was com-
patable with the plan of a mere Hand-Book for
Visitors;—hence the publication of the following
Work, upon which much pains and considerable
cost have been bestowed, with a view to render it
in some degree worthy the locality which it under-
takes to describe, and the patronage to which it
aspires.

It may be proper here to state that it formed no
part of the original design of the present Volume to
furnish a *History* of Cheltenham, in the proper acceptation of that term. But, seeing that greater
interest naturally attaches to scenes and circum-

stances with which the story of the past has
become associated, a brief review of the leading
events connected with the Rise and Progress of the
Town has been introduced ; and, in order more fully
to exhibit these events in their order of succession,
a Chronological arrangement interspersed with
historical and anecdotal notices will be found ap-
pended to the Work.

For himself the Author claims no merit beyond
that of endeavouring, in a plain and familiar style,
to call attention to the various Institutions and objects of local interest with which the place abounds,
uniformly preferring accuracy of detail to beauty
of composition.   As its publisher, however, he feels
warranted in expressing his conviction that the
Volume here submitted to public criticism, will be
found, as a work of art, superior to any publication of its kind that has ever issued from the Cheltenham press.

Montpellier Library,
    June 1, 1843.

ILLUSTRATIONS.

PLAN
of the
TOWN OF
CHELTENHAM
1843

REFERENCE
1 S. Mary's Church
2 Trinity Ch.
3 S. John's Ch.
4 S. James's Ch.
5 S. Paul's Ch.
6 Christchurch
7 S. Philip's Church
8 Montpellier Spa
9 Kings Old Wells
10 Pittville Spa
11 Cambray Ch.
12 Assembly Rooms
13 Hospital
14 Literary Institution
15 Subscription & Baths
16 Masonic Hall
17 Police Barracks
18 Post Office
19 Market

CHELTENHAM.

CHAPTER I.

POLITICAL AND PAROCHIAL HISTORY.

*Cheltenham—Notices of its early History—Ancient and present Manor—
Discovery of Mineral Waters—Rise and progress of the Town—Bays
Hill Lodge—The Town in 1780—First Local Acts of Parliament—
Visit of King George the Third—Montpellier and Suffolk Properties—
Chalybeate Spas—Present State—Political Privileges—Population—
Rates, Assessments, &c.*

CHELTENHAM has, since the commencement of the present
century, attained to so great a celebrity, and has become,
consequently, a place of so much importance, even in a
national point of view, that the " tales " of its " early
ages " have frequently formed the subjects of ingenious
speculation and learned enquiry. Hence the attention of
the antiquary has been repeatedly directed to the investigation of its history, and divers pens have been employed
in tracing its rise and progress from a state of comparative
insignificance up to that of one of the most flourishing and
populous boroughs in the kingdom. The same laudable
curiosity which prompts the " learned author " to inquire
into events remote and well nigh forgotten, characterizes
(though, happily, in a less intense degree) every educated

B

and intelligent person; and the pleasures which are derived
from extending the sphere of knowledge, and acquiring
fresh information, prove an ample reward for the labours
undergone in qualifying the mind for their adequate enjoyment. When, therefore, a stranger visits any particular
place, with the local history of which he is unacquainted,
he naturally becomes desirous of knowing something about
it; and should he chance to observe any building differing
in appearance from those by which it is surrounded, such,
for instance, as a church, a pump-room, or the ruin of an
ancient castle, he feels anxious to gain more information
concerning them than it is possible for him to attain by
merely gazing at their outer walls. He enquires into the
purposes for which they were originally erected, by whom,
and the mutations which in the lapse of ages they may
have, peradventure, undergone. If he be of a poetical
temperament, these enquiries have a more than ordinary
interest to him; for he would fain identify his own with
the feelings and emotions of other days, and recal the
dreams of by-gone generations. Or, on the other hand,
should our stranger be a votary of pleasure, desiring rather
to mingle in the gaieties of the living, than to share in
imagination the " sports and pastimes" of the dead, he
is no less anxious to learn how these his desires may be
most easily gratified, and where he is to seek those amusements which are congenial to his habits and inclinations.
Hence, he feels the want of a Guide who shall conduct
him to the various places which merit his particular attention, and afford all necessary information for his introduction into new scenes of life and action. The aim of
the following pages, therefore, will be to supply, so far
as " Cheltenham and its environs" are concerned, this
desideratum, by pointing out those objects which seem

best calculated to excite a stranger's interest, and thereby contribute to his gratification. But, before we proceed to develop this portion of our plan, it will, doubtless, be expected that we should give some sketch, however brief, of the early history of the Town and Manor, which we will, therefore, in as few words as possible, endeavour to do.

Utter obscurity rests upon the "infant days" of our now highly favoured town, and no trace of its "birth and parentage" can be discovered through the darkness and gloom of the past. But little, save vague and unsatisfactory conjecture, exists with respect to the derivation of its name, a subject upon which, as antiquaries are by no means agreed, we deem it quite unnecessary to trouble the reader at any length. Atkyns affirms it to have been derived from that of the brook *Chilt*, but of this word he does not give the etymology. Rudder is of opinion that " Cheltenham" comes from the Saxon *Chylt*, clay, and *Ham*, a house, or village; and other writers have imagined other derivations—but happily the question is one of no very great importance. From the military and other remains which are still in existence on the surrounding heights, and from the coins, &c., which, at various times, have been discovered in the immediate neighbourhood, it may be very reasonably inferred that the scite was well known to the Romans, whose stations at *Corinium*, the present Cirencester, and *Glevum* or Gloucester, were connected together by the great Roman road, which passed within a few miles of the place. Nor is it probable that the early inhabitants of Britain had neglected to take advantage of a spot so perfectly well-adapted for permanent location as that which the situation of Cheltenham presented. But as no mention of it is made in any of the old Roman or British Itineraries, we must be content to remain in entire ignorance of its very existence for the first thousand years of the Christian era!

The earliest authentic notice* we meet with of the town and manor of Cheltenham, is in the Domesday Book, where it is called *Chinteneham*, and is recorded to have belonged, in former times, to Edward the Confessor; to whom it paid nine pounds five shillings in money, and " three thousand loaves for the dogs!" At this time the manor contained only about 850 acres, while at present it embraces the whole of the township, consisting of nearly 1200 acres, beside the hamlets of Arle, Alstone, and Westal, Naunton and Sandford, together with the adjoining parishes of Charlton, Leckhampton, and Swindon. After the conquest it became the property of the Norman William, in whose reign the payments in money and kind were increased to £20, twenty cows, and twenty hogs, with 16s. in lieu of the " 3000 loaves for the dogs." The successors of the Conqueror, though they repeatedly disposed of it to their followers, appear still to have retained the rights of seigniory in their own hands.

During the unsettled and turbulent reigns of the middle ages, the place is frequently mentioned as being in the possession of sundry barons and bishops, who either by the exchange of other property, or else by specific grants, obtained it from the crown. In 1252, Henry III. conveyed it to the priory of Fescamp, in Normandy, in lieu of lands which were assigned him in Winchester and Rye;—and

* Tanner, in his *Notitia Monastica*, mentions the existence of a monastry in Cheltenham, as early as 803; in which year Denebert, Bishop of Worcester, claimed from it and Beckford, as their diocesan, a certain feast or annual payment, which the Bishop of Hereford (who, it would seem, in former times, possessed the monastry) refused to grant. It was, however, arranged that the Bishop of Worcester should receive the feast from the monasteries of Cheltenham and Beckford alternately.—*See Moreau's Cheltenham Guide.*

from this period till the time of the gallant " Harry of Monmouth," it remained in possession of the church. In his reign, the Parliament having passed an Act declaring the property of all alien monasteries to be vested in the crown, Henry became seised of the manor and hundred of Cheltenham, which, however, he did not long retain in his own hands, but granted it to the nunnery of Sion, in Middlesex, in whose safe keeping it remained until the spirit of the reformation, and the caprice of Henry VIII. uniting to produce the dissolution of all monastic institutions in this country, caused it again, and finally, to revert to the crown. That the town of Cheltenham, during the period which has just passed under review, possessed rights and privileges which it now no longer enjoys, is sufficiently manifest from the fact of Queen Elizabeth excusing William Norwood, who then held the manor, from the trouble and expense of sending two members to Parliament, as had been the practice in former times.

In 1618, Charles Prince of Wales sold the manor of Cheltenham for the sum of twelve hundred pounds, to John Dutton, Esq., of Sherborne, in whose descendants all manorial rights have ever since been vested.* At the time this Prince disposed of his interests in Cheltenham to the ancestor of the present Lord Sherborne, the town itself must have been a place of some importance, since, in the reign of Charles the Second (A.D. 1666) its population amounted to fifteen hundred souls; a number by no means inconsiderable, when we take into account the sanguinary character of the civil wars which had intervened and resulted in the interregnum; for there is no reason to imagine that Cheltenham escaped its ruinous and

* The covenants of this sale were not ratified until 1628, 3rd of Charles I.

depopulating effects; especially as we find it at one period garrisoned by a royalist cavalry brigade, under the command of Lords Chandos and Grandison, who were, however, obliged to evacuate the place on the approach of the Earl of Essex with the parliamentary forces, which took possession of, and encamped in the town on its march to Gloucester, at that time besieged by the army of the king.

During the first half of the eighteenth century the town would seem to have made but little if any progress—the population remaining stationary, or very nearly so. Even the discovery of its mineral springs, which took place in 1716, produced, for the first twenty-five years, no appreciable increase in the number of its inhabitants. The publication of several works on the medical properties of the Waters, particularly the treatise of Dr. Short, in 1740, appears, however, to have tended materially to bring the place into note, to which the chemical investigations of Senckenberg and Mortimer, published in the Philosophical transactions of the following year, still further contributed. The attention of the medical profession being, by these means, called to the importance of the Cheltenham Waters, they were soon extensively recommended for the cure of numerous disorders, and the place consequently, became much resorted to by invalids; for whose accommodation many additions and improvements were annually made. Among these were the erection of several lodging houses, the conversion of the meadows around the Spa into walks and pleasure grounds, and the planting of the famous avenue of Elms in 1739.

About the same time a Lady Stapleton had built for her private residence, a spacious mansion, a short distance west of the church, overlooking, in the direction of the

Wells, the meadow, then called *Church-mead*, and through which, in after time, two gravelled footpaths conducted—the

one to the bridge, at the lower end of St. George's Place, & the other to the entrance of the Old Well Walk, which was entered over a slight

CHURCH-MEAD AND THE GREAT HOUSE.

drawbridge here thrown across the Chelt. This mansion, then called the " Great House," was, after her ladyship's death, converted into a boarding house, which for many years was the scene of the principal amusements then in fashion—dancing, card, and tea-drinking parties assembling there every evening in the week, Mondays excepted.* This was, of course, previous to the establishment of any Assembly Rooms in the town; for on the appointment of a Master of the Ceremonies, and the introduction of regular Public Balls, the dancing and card parties of the Great House were necessarily merged into the latter. It continued, however, to be used as a Boarding House down to 1838—its proximity to the Spas, and, at the same time, its contiguity to the Church and the High Street, rendering it, during the season, much frequented for a period of full half a century. But in the year last named, the original Boarding House, together with the Clarence Hotel, an important adjunct to that building, were, on the opening of the Queen's Hotel, obliged to be closed—Mr.

* The Cheltenham Guide of 1741, p. 31.

Liddell, the then tenant of the former, becoming lessee of the latter; and concentrating there the business and connections of both establishments.

A curious old sketch, taken by one of the Ladies Somerset of that day, from the south window of Lady Stapleton's residence, in the year 1748, and still in the possession of W. N. Skillicorne, Esq., conveys a graphic view of the Old Well walk, shortly after its formation, with the Pump Room and premises then in existence, as well as of fields and meadows now covered over with buildings of surpassing splendour; and showing also, in the distance, the spire and Court House of Leckhampton, with the Painswick hills rising immediately in front—the entrance into Church-meadow being seen in the left-hand corner of the foreground.   According to this drawing it would seem that

CHELTENHAM—OLD WELLS, 1748.

not more than four houses of any description were then scattered over a tract of country which subsequently became the scites of the Crescent, the Promenades, the extensive districts of the Montpellier, Suffolk, Bays Hill, and Lansdown estates, with their populous surrounding neighbourhoods. A few detached cottages rose slowly into existence to the south of the church, but no building of any magnitude was erected after that of Lady Stapleton's, until 1781, when Bays Hill Lodge was built for the Earl of Faulconberg, on the brow of the hill, two fields west of the Spa.

A circumstance of some moment, as indicating the rising importance of the town, particularly in the estimation of the fashionable world, now took place: this was none other than the appointment of a Master of the Ceremonies. The gentleman chosen to this office was Simon Moreau, Esq., of Bath, who, in the summer of 1780, was installed first M.C. of Cheltenham—the number of visitors being, in that year, 374. This number continued annually increasing, and at the close of the next decade the visitors are reported to have amounted to 1100.

The first " Cheltenham Guide, or Useful Companion in a Journey of Health and Pleasure," was published in London in 1781;* and this describes the town as consisting, at that time, of " one regular, spacious and handsome street, about a mile in length "—the houses being " chiefly of brick." This " handsome street " was, however, " encumbered with certain old coarse buildings, supported on stone pillars, called the Corn Market and Butter Cross," and " another below them which neither had nor merited a name. A little farther down was a kind of cage or prison, built of stone, and not unsuitably decorated with the inscription in front—Do well, and fear not." To this

* In this same year there was also published, in London, a small volume, entitled " The Cheltenham Guide, or Memoirs of the B— H— R— D. Family continued in a Series of Poetical Epistles; by Anstey, the author of the famous New Bath Guide ; but possessing no particular merit.

description the writer adds—"It is hoped that objects so very unsightly will soon be removed, and the necessary accommodations for marketting, &c., placed on some more retired and convenient spot." A hope (as will be seen) which was shortly realized.

Down to this period of its history there was no *direct* communication between Cheltenham and Lodon, but "a stage coach holding six," and "a diligence carrying three passengers," which travelled between the metropolis and Gloucester, halted to change horses at Frogmill, whence passengers to Cheltenham were "accommodated with good post chaises at a small expense." The London post arrived and departed thrice a-week, and there was one "cross-post" to Gloucester, which came and went a like number of times. Such were its means of communication and intercommunication in 1781.

We have next to notice the introduction of a measure productive of the most beneficial results, and which conferred upon Cheltenham a political importance hitherto unenjoyed. This was the passing, in 1786, of an Act of Parliament for the paving, lighting, and internal government of the town, and the appointment of Commissioners for carrying the same into effect. The authorities thus constituted immediately commenced the work of improvement. In the July of this year the "old market house" and "Butter Cross" were, by their direction, taken down, and the materials sold for the sum of £64 19s.; and in lieu thereof a new market house was (Sept. 27) ordered to be erected on the site of the "old Blind House and Prison." The first foot-pavement was, in the following month, directed to be put down, 4½ feet wide "in Cheltenham Street;" and on the 16th of January, 1787, an order was given for putting up one hundred and twenty lamps, at twenty-five yards apart, which were to be lighted in the autumn and winter months only. The contract for this first lighting of our town provided that the lamps should burn till midnight; but " when the moon rises at ten o'clock or before then, the lamps are to burn bright only one hour after the moon rises." Such a regulation cannot but raise a smile when viewed in contrast with the splendid manner of lighting the High Street of Cheltenham in the present day, when, instead of one hundred and twenty flittering oil lamps burning till midnight, and for a few months only, there are upwards of one hundred gas lamps constantly burning from dusk till dawn the whole year through. The Commissioners of Paving and Lighting undertook many other improvements, proceeding steadily in the administration of their duties, bringing the internal economy of the town under a better system of regulation than it had previously known, and preparing it for that exaltation to which it was rapidly hastening.

The year immediately preceding (1785) that in which the first Commissioners' Act was obtained, an Act had been passed for amending the Turnpike roads passing out of Cheltenham to Gloucester, Burford, Cirencester, Bath, and other places with which lines of communication had, at various times and under different circumstances, been opened.* These legislative enactments for the improvement of the town and its approaches, was, doubtless, productive of the most beneficial results, and contributed to increase the number of its annual visitors, which are stated, in 1784, to have considerably exceeded a thousand.

But the event which, of all others, contributed most to the advancement of Cheltenham, was the visit of his Majesty King George the Third, in the summer of 1788,

* *Moreau's Tour to the Royal Spa at Cheltenham.* Edit. 1797, p. 38.

accompanied by his Queen and other members of the Royal
Family.   His Majesty having been advised by his physicians to drink the Spa Waters, did so for the space of a
month, namely, from the 14th of July to the 16th of

Aug.; during which time
the Royal Family resided
at Bays Hill Lodge, the
seat of Earl Faulcon-
berg, to which very con-
siderable additions were
made with a view to their
better   accommodation.
During his stay in Chel-
tenham the King passed
much time in public, fre-

BAYS HILL LODGE.

quently joining in the promenades—for there were musical
promenades in those days,—visiting most of the places of
amusement or celebrity in the town and neighbourhood, and
receiving addresses from various corporate bodies.

While resident at Bays Hill Lodge, his Majesty directed
a well to be sunk in the grounds about a hundred yards
distant from the house, there being a scarcity of water for
the domestic purposes of his establishment.   But having
gone down between fifty and sixty feet into the blue clay,
instead of a fresh water spring a strong saline one was the
result; and the supply from this, which was called the
King's Well, proved, for many years, much more abundant
than that obtained from any of the other wells on the Bays
Hill estate.   This supply, however, after a time, gradually
failed, and the King's Well was, in consequence, finally
closed about the year 1812.   The accidental discovery of
this new well was, at the particular period of its occurrence,
of considerable importance, there having been, for some

time, an insufficiency of mineral water for the constantly increasing number of drinkers—the supply of the Old Wells being frequently exhausted at a very early hour in the morning. In order to economise the supply as much as possible, the King issued his royal command that the Wells should be shut altogether on Sundays, during the period of his stay in the place.*

The manifest improvement which his Majesty's health underwent, and the presence of the court for so long a time, could not fail giving a fresh impulse to the prosperity of our rising watering place, which these fortunate events may be considered to have now fully and fairly established. The Spa at which his Majesty drank the Waters with such beneficial results, was henceforth distinguished as the *Royal Wells:* and in commemoration of this auspicious visit, S. Moreau, Esq., the M.C., had a suit- able medal struck, having, on one side, a figure of Hygeia, holding a profile of his Majesty, and on

GEORGE III. COMMEMORATION MEDAL.

the reverse a representation of the building covering the Well, each surrounded by an appropriate inscription.

From the year of King George's visit to the close of the eighteenth century no event of moment occurred. The town kept steadily advancing in public estimation, and the number of visitors, most of whom came to drink the Waters, had, from 374 in 1780, increased to nearly two thousand in 1800. The season, as it is termed, lasted four months, from the 1st of June to the 30th of September; and during its continuance the lodging houses throughout

* Fothergill on the Cheltenham Waters. Edition 1788, p. 99.

the town were charged double what they were in the spring and autumn.* It is amusing enough to contrast the state of certain local matters at the period now under notice, with their improved condition in the present day. In those good old times the mail, which left London at half-past six, p.m., arrived in Cheltenham about eleven the following morning; and the letters were delivered at the office-window about twelve o'clock. The return mail left at a quarter past four—the letter-box closing as half-past three. Now, the mail which leaves London at nine, p.m., arrives in Cheltenham at three a.m.—not leaving, on its return, until eleven at night. In the year 1800 the celebrated Dr. Jenner was the only resident physician in the town—though during the season other members of the faculty came over from Bath:—five surgeons and apothecaries, and one chemist and druggist, completed the " medical staff." In 1842 there were, according to the Directory for that year, twenty physicians and thirty surgeons, and between thirty and forty chemists and druggists. The public entertainments of the epoch, which we have just reviewed, consisted of balls, card parties, and theatrical representations; all of which, though of nightly occurrence, would seem to have been liberally supported.

The commencement of the present century proved the beginning of a new era to Cheltenham, the population of which, according to the census of 1801, was 3076, and the number of inhabited houses 710. There were also fifteen houses building. From the parish registers we find the number of baptisms were eighty-seven, the marriages twenty-four, and burials forty-seven.† In this year the Delabere property, now called " the Montpellier," was purchased by Mr. H. Thompson. It consisted of between

* *Chelt. Annuaire,* 1838, p. 111.   † *Ibid.*

three and four hundred acres, immediately contiguous to the Bays Hill estate, and extending from beyond Lansdown to the Bath road and Sandford fields. A short time prior to Mr. Thompson's purchase, the Earl of Suffolk had bought about thirty acres adjoining, for which he gave the sum of £2800. St. James's church, Suffolk Square, and Suffolk Lawn, now stand upon portions of Lord Suffolk's land.*

Mr. Thompson, being a gentleman of great enterprise, immediately proceeded to turn his purchases to account; and having sunk a number of wells, discovered several varieties of mineral waters. He erected for himself a handsome residence, which he named Hygeia House,† now called Victoria House, near the Bath road; and shortly after built public Baths hard by. He also formed roads and planted walks and pleasure drives; and disposing of numerous plots of ground for building purposes, developed the resources of his estate to an extent that surprised, while it called forth the admiration of the speculators of the previous century. As we shall have to speak of Mr. Thompson's improvements hereafter, when we come to treat of the Spas, we need not further dwell upon them here.

In 1803 the first Chalybeate spring was discovered in a meadow near the Chelt, at the back of the present Belle

---

* *Cheltenham Annuaire* for 1837, p. 96.

† It was in the grounds immediately around Hygeia House that Mr. Thompson's first experimental borings were made, and a number of fine saline springs being the result, he promptly made arrangements for affording to the public the benefit of his discoveries; and it was, consequently, hence that the now celebrated Montpellier Spas date their origin. The Waters of the Wells here referred to, though no longer required for the drinkers, are still, we believe, used for the manufacture of the Cheltenham Salts—being conveyed in pipes to the Laboratory for that purpose.

Vue Place, and in 1807 the Cambray Chalybeate. The former was much frequented for some years, but has long since been wholly disused; the latter is still in existence. In 1809 the first Montpellier Pump Room was opened; and in the same year a mineral spring was discovered and a Spa established at Alstone, which, however, never attained to much note; and was altogether abandoned in 1820.* The establishment of four new Spas in the short space of six years affords unerring indications of the rapidly increasing reputation of the place, and the building, simultaneously with these, of a Theatre in Cambray meadow (1805), the publication of the first newspaper (1809), the construction of a tram-road to Gloucester (1809), the erection of new and spacious Assembly Rooms (1810), and the commencement of several other important undertakings, including the Crescent and the Colonnade, furnish corroborative evidence of the same fact, and prepare us to learn that in the year 1811, when the census was again taken, that the population of Cheltenham had more than doubled itself—the number of its inhabitants being then 8325, and its inhabited houses 1556.

Through the progress of the next ten years the spirit of enterprise held pace with the increasing celebrity of the Mineral Waters, and numerous improvements and additions were annually made in the town to meet the wants of the times, and afford accommodation to the strangers who now resorted hither from all parts of the world.

* This Spa was situate near the present Alstone Mill. Its waters were analyzed by Accum in 1810; but, either from its inconvenient locality, or some other cause, it never attained to much celebrity. One singular circumstance connected with its history is, that, as a last effort to obtain support, the waters were carried through the town in the morning, in a water-cart, provided for that purpose. This was about the year 1820.—*Cheltenham Annuaire*, for 1837.

During this period several valuable institutions were established. A new road to Bath was opened through Cambray (1813). The Assembly Rooms of 1810 were found to be much too small, and larger and handsomer ones were speedily erected (1816). The Montpellier Pump Room, now growing rapidly into fashion, was considerably enlarged (1817). The principal streets of the town were lighted with gas in 1818. In the same year the Grand Promenade, leading from the High Street, was formed and planted, and a new and elegant Pump Room erected at its upper end. This was called at first *The Sherborne Spa*, but afterwards changed its name to *The Imperial*, and for a

THE SHERBORNE OR IMPERIAL SPA.

time met with considerable support: but this declining, the building was taken down in 1838, and the Queen's Hotel erected on its site. The walks and drives attached

c

to this Spa were, for many years after the trees had attained their growth, among the most beautiful in Cheltenham. The Crescent—the building of which had been

THE CRESCENT, IN 1812.

commenced a few years before, was completed early in the period now under review; and in the year 1812, Church Meadow, upon which this un-

dertaking was planned, presented, in consequence, a widely different appearance to that which it exhibited in 1803, when the view, shown in a preceding page, was sketched. Public Races were established in 1819. Bands of Music were engaged to perform daily at the different Spas, and a variety of novel and fashionable amusements introduced, with a view of contributing to the gaiety and attractiveness of the place by increasing the pleasures and gratifications of the visitors, and thereby inducing numbers of them to become permanent residents—a result which followed to a very large extent: and at the taking of the census of 1821, the population had, consequently, increased to 13,388, and the inhabited houses to 2411.

From 1821 to the date of the next population returns the town underwent very extensive alterations. This period may, indeed, be distinguished as, above all others, that in which Cheltenham most rapidly developed its resources, and attained to a celebrity which it has not even since surpassed, though its borders have been greatly enlarged, and the number of its inhabitants mightily increased. Its

Spas were, during the epoch here referred to, resorted to by thousands; and the attractive character of its amusements caused them to be as eagerly sought after by the healthy, as its waters were by the invalid. New lines of communication were opened with several of the principal cities and towns of the kingdom, with which, previously, no direct means of intercourse existed; and numerous coaches were started, and facilities of intercommunication established, which rendered Cheltenham easy of access to multitudes, who before had, from the expense or tediousness of the intervening journies, been deterred from visiting the place. The rapidly increasing extension of the town, consequent upon these circumstances, demanded still increased accommodation of a public as well as private character; these the enterprize and speculating tendencies of the period were sufficiently prompt in providing. The market-house, built in the centre of the High Street, in 1787, was removed, and more spacious and commodious buildings, with a covered Arcade leading to them, erected by Lord Sherborne in 1822. In the following year the first new church—that of Trinity—was completed. A public company was incorporated for supplying the town with water in 1824, and in the same year a second Cheltenham newspaper was started. The Pump Room and pleasure grounds of the Pittville Spa were commenced in 1825—in which year St. James's church was also begun; and early in the following spring the Montpellier Rotunda upreared its beautiful structure, as if called into existence by the wand of an enchanter; and the field opposite was laid out as gardens and pleasure grounds, which, however, were not opened to the public till three years after, by which time also the Pittville Pump Room was completed and put forth its claims to public support. In the year 1829, St.

John's, the third additional church erected in Cheltenham within the space of seven years, was consecrated to public worship, and several schools and benevolent institutions, including the first Infant School, were established about the same time. A new road to Gloucester, starting from the back of the Montpellier Spa, had been made during the period now under review, and a considerable tract of land on its right converted into building ground, upon which several large houses, on the Lansdowne estate, had been already erected. The upper and lower Promenades, Cambray, Rodney and Oriel Terraces, and Oriel Place, with the fine rows of buildings on the right and left of the London road, and a number of other streets, branching north and south out of the High Street, as well as a great many detached houses on the Pittville and Montpellier estates, were either wholly or in part built between 1821 and 1831. In which latter year the Parliamentary return reported the resident population to be 22,942; or, according to another return, which, in all probability, included the population of the immediate suburbs, to be 26,574; and the number of the inhabited houses 4018.

In the year immediately following that of taking the census above noticed, Cheltenham, in common with other large towns of the empire, acquired a political importance which it had not before enjoyed, at least not since the reign of Queen Elizabeth, and, by the Reform Act of 1831, was constituted a borough, entitled to send one member to Parliament. The electors of that year chose for their representative the Hon. C. F. Berkeley, the brother of Earl Fitzhardinge, to whose return, on this occasion, there was no opposition. The same gentleman was returned to the four succeeding Parliaments—though not on each occasion, as on the first, without opposition.

The growth and progress of the town through the decennial period, extending from 1831 to 1841, equalled, and in some respects even surpassed, that of the epoch immediately preceding, distinguished as this had been for its many and valuable improvements. New buildings arose with a rapidity perfectly surprising: upon the Lansdown estate alone above one hundred and twenty houses were erected, and nearly, if not quite, as many on the properties north of the High Street, and contiguous to the Pittville Spa; Imperial Square, the east side of the Promenade, Suffolk Square, Park Place, Tivoli, and other ranges of private residences, advanced towards completion within the period; and before its close the Park and Bays Hill estates were converted into building grounds— many excellent houses being immediately erected thereupon. Three new churches—St. Paul's, Christ Church, and St. Phillips, in Leckhampton parish—were built and opened for the accommodation of their respective districts. Two additional newspapers were started, a Literary and Philosophical Institution founded, and various additions made to the public establishments of the town—the internal economy and regulation of which underwent simultaneous improvement.

In 1841, when the census was again taken, the population of the parish of Cheltenham was found to amount to 31,391, and the number of inhabited houses to 5664, being an increase since the commencement of the century of 28,315 in the former, and of 1646 in the latter.* But the continued prosperity of Cheltenham cannot be fully estimated by the increase of its population alone. In order to form an adequate conception of the present wealth and condition of the town it will be necessary to furnish a few

* There were also 629 houses uninhabited, and 139 building.

other statistical items, and,—where this can be done,—to contrast them with similar items at former periods.

The total value of the property of Cheltenham, estimated by an assessment of the houses and lands throughout the parish, made in the summer of 1841, amounts to £189,469 6s. 8d.   Upon this a poor-rate of ninepence in the pound produced the sum of £7105 0s. 6d.   A rate of ninepence upon houses and one shilling upon land, ordered in 1806, yielded only £299 2s. 8d.*   At that time the Plough Hotel was assessed at £65 a-year, and Mr. Gardner's Brewery at £18, while at the present time the assessment of the former stands at £1260, and of the latter at £516—so greatly has the value of property increased in the space of thirty-five years.†

Some curious notices of the past and present state of the town were published in the *Cheltenham Annuaire* for 1838—of which the following may be taken as an example:—" Upon that portion of the Delabere estate, purchased by the late Henry Thompson, comprising the present Lansdown, Montpellier, Suffolk, and Sandford districts of Cheltenham, there were in the year 1801, when the purchase in question was made, but *two houses*—Gallipot Farm, since converted into Suffolk House, and Westhall.   Upon this self-same portion of property there are now between *eight and nine hundred*, a large proportion of which are quite of the first class, which, according to the average number of five and a half persons to each house, would alone give a population of between four and five thousand."   As a parallel illustration, it may be mentioned that in 1806, when a survey was made of the parish, there appeared to have been but five buildings in the whole

* *Cheltenham Annuaire*, 1838—p. 112.
† The Queen's Hotel, in 1841, was assessed at £1457.

of the hamlets of Westal, Naunton, and Sandford; namely, Gallipot and Sandford farms, a cottage, occupied by Lady Mary Lindsay, Hygeia House, and the Saline Bath, then newly erected by Mr. Thompson. A careful and accurate census was, for parochial purposes, taken of these same hamlets in the Jan. of 1842, when it was ascertained that the number of houses were 1281,* and the population 6109.†

No laboured examination into the details of the rise and progress of Cheltenham, would convey to the mind a more satisfactory notion thereof than the statistical views above exhibited. In them we behold at a glance the importance to which the place has attained. Nor can we wonder at its proud pre-eminence, when we reflect upon the many causes which have been in operation to produce this effect. The principle of these are, no doubt, referable to the superior natural advantages which the town enjoys, and a few of which will be noticed more at large in the ensuing chapter. These, however, form not the only ones possessed by Cheltenham over and above those of most other towns in the kingdom. Its advantages in many other respects are neither few nor unimportant, and hold out strong inducements to persons of fortune to settle here. It is abundantly supplied with all the necessaries and luxuries of life, and, generally speaking, at a reasonable rate. House rent, which was some years ago higher than in the generality of country towns, has been rapidly accommodating itself to the average of other places; and in many instances is now even considerably lower. The local rates are, on the whole, extremely moderate—particularly the poor-rates, the number of poor in Cheltenham dependant upon parochial relief, being much smaller in proportion to

---

* Inhabited 1163 } Total 1281.   † Males   2330 } Total 6109.
  Unhabited 118 }   Females 2779 }

the aggregate of the population, than in almost any other town. The Highway and the Commissioners' rates for defraying the charges of paving, lighting, and cleansing the town, and for the general purposes of its internal regulation and economy, average together about eight-pence in the pound upon the poor-rate assessment. There are usually two rates a-year. The church-rates seldom exceed three farthings in the pound, and the whole parish is tythe-free.

We have thus endeavoured to present the stranger with a succint account of the present state of Cheltenham, politically considered; and now, passing over all minor points of enquiry in reference thereto, we shall proceed to examine two or three particulars connected with its Natural History.

The better to exhibit the ratio of increase which Cheltenham has undergone since the commencement of the present century, we insert the following tabular view of the population.

In 1801 the number of its Inhabitants was 3076
1811   8325
1821   13,388
1831   22,942
1841   31,391

CHAP. II.

Geographical situation of Cheltenham—The River Chelt—Peculiarities of Climate — Prevailing Winds—Vegetation — The Nightingale — Rare Plants—Geology—Subsoil of the Town—Oolitic, Lias, and Marl formations—Fossils—Origin of Mineral Waters.

To most persons who visit Cheltenham on account of their health, the Political History of the place will doubtless be considered of infinitely less importance than its natural, especially as in the latter respect it possesses one peculiarity at least not common to other towns;—we allude to its mineral waters. As far as this requires illustration, it may be expected that we should devote a few pages to the subject; and we purpose doing so. But before we enter upon the examination which it involves, we may be permitted to notice a few other points of minor importance, which legitimately present themselves for inclusion under the head of Natural History.

According to the most accurate calculations the parish church of St. Mary's, Cheltenham, is situated exactly 51° 51′ north latitude, and 2° 51′ west longitude. The town is distant from London, by the coach roads, 95 miles *via* Uxbridge, and 97 *via* Henley. Its level above the sea is about 100 feet;* many of its recently erected portions

---

* According to the calculations made in 1834 by Mr. S. Moss, the base of St. Mary's church is exactly 195 feet above the level of low water mark at Sharp-

are, however, considerably more than this, especially the new buildings round Montpellier, which rise from seventy to ninety feet above the bed of the river Chelt at Lower Alstone Mill.

Those who have been accustomed to associate the presence of broad streams with their ideas of populous towns or rich scenery, have sometimes urged against Cheltenham its want of water—and yet it has its river! which, though not conferring commercial or manufacturing importance on the place, or visibly improving the general effect of the landscape, is yet essentially conducive to the health of the population and the fertility of the land along its borders. The *Chelt* originates in several small rivulets which rise in the hills around Dowdeswell, and flowing thence through Charlton Park, enters the parish of Cheltenham near Sandford Mill, on the old Bath road, whence its course meanders through the low grounds at the back of Keynsham Bury and Belle Vue Place, to the mill hard by. From this spot the stream, in former times, dispersed itself along several courses; when swollen by rains, frequently flowing down the High Street, where, at certain distances apart, it was crossed by stepping stones. For the last half century, however, it has been confined to its present channel, running under the Bath road, across Wellington Street, Rodney Terrace, and the Promenade, down to the bottom of St. George's Place, where it re-appears in sight, after having held the course above indicated almost wholly concealed from view, having been built over from time to time, as the successive alterations and improvements of the town rendered necessary more convenient approaches

ness Point. That adopted in the text, is according to the trigonometrical survey, as given in Mr. Murchison's " Outline of the Geology of the Neighbourhood of Cheltenham."

and communications with its different districts, than were
afforded by the narrow bridges which formerly crossed the
stream, and which were, consequently, one after another
taken down. Among the most ancient and curious of
these, was one of stone, which carried the road from
the Crescent to Westall
Green, crossing the stream
not far from the entrance
to the Old Well Walk; and
a sketch of which, made
just before its removal,
shows it to have possessed
some features, at least, of

OLD BRIDGE, 1821.

rustic beauty: on this bridge being taken down the river
here was arched over to the level of the carriage road.
The *Chelt* empties itself into the Severn, at Wainlode
bridge, near to the entrance of the coal canal which
comes up to Coomb Hill, and distant from Cheltenham
seven miles.

The observations of meteorologists demonstrate that
the climate of Cheltenham differs in no essential particular,
as to its general character, from that of other places simi-
larly situated, though the operation of certain local causes,
to be shortly noticed, renders it sensibly milder. The
average temperature, as indicated by carefully registered
observations, continued through a series of seven years,
extending from 1830 to 1837, may be stated as 50·26 degrees—the range of the thermometer being, during the
same period, 65° mean maximum, and 21·3° mean minimum, which, as compared with the results of corresponding
observations registered at Edmonton, indicate in Cheltenham a general temperature less subject to extremes of
heat and cold than that which the climate of London un-

dergoes.* And though the metropolis itself may, according to Dr. Jameson's tables, appear to be about 1½ degrees warmer than Cheltenham; yet as this difference must be wholly the effect of artificial causes, arising chiefly from a confined and heated atmosphere, it is perfectly obvious that London can lay no claim to any natural advantages upon the score of superior mildness.

Surrounded on the north-east, east, and south-east, by the lofty range of the Cotteswold hills, the town is sheltered, to a very considerable extent, from the winds which blow from those points; or at least is not subjected to their severity: while being open to the south and west it is proportionably exposed to the winds which proceed from those quarters—these latter, accordingly, are found to prevail in the proportion of two to one throughout the year. Hence it was found, in 1837, that, taking the average of the winds which had been registered during the preceding seven years, the east wind had blown twenty-eight and the west wind forty-five days; the north thirty-five and the south fifty days: and while the north-east winds had prevailed but thirty-three days those from the south-west were equal to ninety-seven days each year. This prevalence of the warm winds has the effect of raising the general temperature of the climate; but this tendency becomes, in turn, modified by the circumstance of those winds, in their journies hitherward, blowing over the Welsh mountains and the Bristol Channel, and being thereby slightly cooled. But as they are milder so are they also moister than those of the north and east; and their progress eastward being

* See the Tables published in the *Cheltenham Annuaire*, 1837, and compiled from data furnished by Mr. S. Moss, who, for many years of his residence in Cheltenham, kept a daily register of the winds and weather; and which are still the only meteorological *authorities* upon which any reliance can be placed.

often arrested by the neighbouring hills, the consequences are evidenced in more frequent showers than fall in situations farther inland. " But if in Cheltenham we have fewer *bright* days than in France, we have also fewer *rainy* ones than in Devonshire." The average annual fall of rain in Cheltenham is about 33 inches.

But not to rest our assertions upon the testimony of meteorological calculations alone, the observer of nature will find abundant evidence of a mild climate in the forward state of spring; the general healthy appearance of vegetation around the neighbourhood, and numberless other unerring indications of that fact. Of these, the early coming of the nightingale deserves to be particularly noticed. During the months of April (the latter end), May, and June, these winged warblers tenant the woods and thickets in every direction round the town; and those who delight to listen to their " wood notes wild," will seldom fail being gratified any evening after sun-set, should they stroll as far as Bennal's wood, about one mile on the Gloucester road, where they usually congregate in great numbers, so great indeed as to have obtained for that spot the name of Nightingale Grove. It may likewise be generally heard in the plantations which border the streamlet at the back of the Park estate, occasionally in the Pittville grounds, and in many other places in the immediate environs of the town. We have listened to its midnight notes, " most musical, most melancholy," in Hatherley lane; and, in the spring of 1841, even so near the " abodes of men " as the corner of the field at the end of Suffolk Lawn.

Naturalists have frequently remarked, that certain birds appear to select their haunts with reference to the habitats of particular plants. That, for example, the nightingale seems to have a preference for those localities where the *bee* and *fly orchis* generally grow. Of this our own neighbourhood affords an illustration—those very rare and beautiful plants being found in the Birdlip and Cranham woods; and—especially the *fly orchis*—in several places around Leckhampton.

Among other scarce and curious plants which grow in our immediate vicinity, the diligent botanist will discover,

The *anemone pulsatilla*, chiefly on the Cotteswold hills.

The purple variety of the *anagallis*, on Cleeve hill and about the Park estate.

The white variety of the *habenaria bifolia*, along the side of the Winchcomb road, Cleeve hill.

The *rubus saxatilis* and *convallaria polygonatum*, in Queen Wood.

The *thlaspi perfoliatum*, at the Seven Wells, and on the banks of the Windrush, near Bourton-on-the-Water. The only habitat of this plant in Britain.

The *lathyrus aphaca*, in the hedge by the side of the footpath, from Marl hill to Prestbury.

The *Euphorbia platyphylla*, at Marl hill.

And in the ponds and ditches of the neighbourhood, particularly on Leigh-common, the fringed buckbean, *menyanthes nymphoides*, and the flowering-rush, *butomus umbellatus*.

Having thus slightly touched upon the natural phenomena peculiar to Cheltenham and its environs, in respect to its situation and climate, as well as its natural history, in the popular acceptation of that term, we will now present our readers with a brief sketch of its Geology, as involving the origin of those mineral waters for which our town has become so universally celebrated.

The subsoil of the whole of the vale of Gloucester, at the eastern extremity of which Cheltenham is situate, consists of what geologists term the *lias*, which, commencing at the base of the Cotteswold hills, spreads over a surface of many miles, extending even to the river Severn. It is upon the hard, stiff, impermeable clay of this formation that the town is built. The clayey nature of this subsoil renders the land heavy and difficult of working for many purposes of agriculture—the loam which covers it rarely exceeding twenty to twenty-four inches in depth (except where artificially formed), and through this alluvium the lias is constantly forcing its way to the surface. This, from the adhesive quality of the soil in wet weather, renders the unstoned roads and thoroughfares unpleasant to travel, particularly for pedestrians; but as all moisture flows readily off, the ground dries again in a remarkably short space of time. Extensive beds of sand and gravel, varying in thickness from one to twenty and even to thirty feet, rest upon the lias in many places in Cheltenham and its neighbourhood. These beds, formed from the detritus of the adjacent hills, have filled up the natural inequalities of the marley substratum; and from their various degrees of thickness produce considerable variety in the nature and properties of the overlying soils. The principal deposits of these sand and gravel washings extend eastward from the Montpellier Gardens and Suffolk Square to the old Bath road, and in a diagonal direction up to the Charlton road, while a much narrower portion stretches westward across Tivoli and Hatherley places, to the course of the stream which flows at the back of the Park. A thin covering of these materials also spreads over many portions of the north side of the High Street, up to the Pittville lake, where the lias again crops out, forming the entire mass of the rising ground upon which the Pump Room is built, and in which the wells which supply that spa with Mineral Waters are sunk.

Mr. Murchison, the learned President of the Geological Society, in an *Outline of the Geology of the Neighbourhood of Cheltenham,* published a few years ago, and which we earnestly recommend to the attentive perusal of every person who feels the least interest in such studies, describes the subsoil of our vicinity as consisting of three grand divisions:—1st. The inferior oolite.—2nd. The lias formation; and, 3rd. The marl, or new red sand-stone. A strata of Stonesfield slate, resting upon a thin layer of Fuller's earth, appears to cap the first of these, upon Sevenhampton Common, *(see (a) of coloured section);* and on the Stow road for miles in extent: below the Fuller's earth the oolitic series commences, and is altogether about 150 feet thick, consisting of—1st. A cream-coloured marl-stone, marked *(a)* in the section. —2nd. *(b)* Upper rag-stone, and thin-bedded oolite; 3rd. *(c)* Freestone, a fine-grained light-coloured oolite; and 4th. *(d)* Lower rag-stone: this lowest member of the inferior oolite is called *pea-grit* by the country people. The organic remains of these oolitic formations are extremely numerous, and some of them very rare. (A list of them appears in the Outline already referred to.) Immediately beneath the pea-grit of the oolite the lias begins. Mr. Murchison informs us that this formation is divided into three parts—1st. The upper lias, or alum-shale, marked *(e)* in the section; 2nd. Marl-stone, marked *(f)*; 3rd. Lower lias-shale, marked *(g)*. In each of which a great variety of peculiar fossils are to be found; some of them *ammonites* of a new species; they are all enumerated in the Outline. The lowest strata consist of a red marl-stone, in which no organic remains have ever

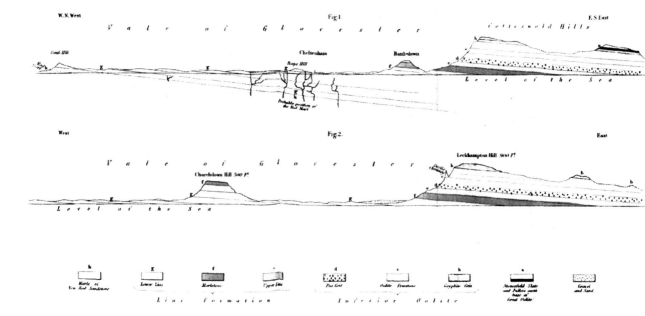

been discovered. This formation shows itself first at
Comb Hill; the whole dipping thence E.S.E. at angles of
from 12° to 15°. Mr. Murchison considers that the
Mineral Waters of Cheltenham have their origin in these
beds of marl-stone, and gives the following highly interesting account of their rise and progress to the surface.

Origin of the Mineral Waters of Cheltenham.

" It is singular that the true nature and geological position of the strata through which these celebrated Waters
rise, should not have been previously pointed out to the
public. In one of the published analyses the Cotteswold
hills are described as being made up of magnesian lime-
stone, and the blue clay, through which the Waters ascend,
is said to cover the lime-stone. That this clay, the lower
lias, passes beneath the calcareous rocks, is a fact now
known to every geologist; and instead of the magnesian
lime-stone (which, if it exists in the district, could only
be found by penetrating to vast depths beneath the surface), the stone of the adjoining hills has been shown
to be the *Inferior Oolite.* Again, in a very recent work,
the production of an able chemist, the Waters are said to
rise through the sand* of the lias. It is therefore desirable
to state distinctly, that the lowest marly and argillaceous
beds of the blue lias formation are really the strata through
which these Waters find their way to the surface. For a
long time after their first discovery, it was the general
belief that they had only one source, but the enterprise
of Mr. Thompson proved this notion to be erroneous. By
numerous sinkings, at depths from 80 to 130 feet, adjacent

* Thermal and Mineral Springs, by Dr. Gairdner, 1832, pp. 419. An
excellent and useful work. The mistake in this case is that of confounding
the superficial sandy detritus of the district, with the formation on which it
rests. The lias shale contains no beds of sand.

D

to and at considerable distances from the old springs, he
established the fact, that many strata were saturated with
water, holding in solution the chloride of sodium and the
sulphate of soda and magnesia, and other mineral substances.

These sinkings were followed by others, at a distance
of nearly two miles from the most distant wells of Montpellier, and the discovery of Waters of nearly the same
composition, has led to the establishment of the New Spa
of Pittville.

It is thus demonstrable, that the mineralization of this
broad expanse of water must be due to causes co-extensive
with the impregnated strata.

From the analyses of these Waters, by several distinguished chemists, it appears that their principle con-
stituents are the chloride of sodium (muriate of soda), or
sea salt, and the sulphate of soda and magnesia. Sulphate
of lime, oxide of iron, and chloride of magnesium, are
present in some wells only, and in much smaller quantities.*
It is remarkable that the proportions in which these substances occur is stated very differently by different chemists,
a circumstance which most probably arises from the Waters
themselves varying in composition. Besides the ingredients just mentioned, Iodine and Bromine have been de-
tected in several of the sources by Dr. Daubeny. That
gentleman was desirous of ascertaining whether these two
active principles, which the French chemists had recently
discovered in modern marine productions, did not also

* The Waters were formerly analysed by Brande and Parkes, subsequently
by Drs. Scudamore and Daubeny. Professor Daniell has examined those of
Pittville, and Mr. Cooper has made a very elaborate analysis of those of Montpellier, with the details of which I am not acquainted. His observations, I
believe, coincide with those of Dr. Daubeny, in the detection of Iodine and
Bromine.

exist in mineral salt waters, issuing from strata which were formed beneath the sea. This examination has established their existence not only in the Waters of Cheltenham, but also in the greater number of the salt-springs of Great Britain.

The great subterranean storehouse of the rock salt and brine springs of England, is the new red sand-stone (or red marl),* a formation which is fully developed in Cheshire and the east of Shropshire. It extends from thence to the S.W. through Worcestershire and Gloucestershire, where its position, with respect to the overlying lias of Cheltenham has been explained. (See fig. 1, coloured diagram.)

Now, if sea salt be the most abundant saline ingredient in all the Mineral Waters of Cheltenham, it is present in still larger quantities in those wells which occur near the western edge of the formation, where the lias forms only a thin covering above the marls of the new red sand-stone. At the new spa near Tewkesbury, where formerly the mineral water at shallow depths below the surface was very slightly saline,·it was recently found to be much more impregnated with salt when the sinking was carried to the depth of 90 feet; and I have no doubt that a similar result would follow, by deepening any of the mineral sources which are so numerous in the Vale of Gloucester, at Walton, the bottom of Church Down Hill, for instance, &c. &c. Again, at Cheltenham, when experimental borings were made by Mr. Thompson, to the depth of 260 feet below the surface, the water of the lowest stratum of marl or clay was found to be more highly charged with the chloride of sodium, or common sea salt, and to contain less of the sulphates, than the existing wells, none of which have been sunk to a greater depth than 130 feet.

* See the Memoir of Dr. Holland, Geol. Trans. vol. I. p. 38, and that of Mr. L. Horner, vol. vi. p. 95, Old Series.

These facts may be accounted for under the supposition, that the source of the saline ingredients of those Waters, is the new red sand-stone, the uppermost strata of which must, from their known inclination, lie at depths of several hundred feet below the town of Cheltenham. The lower part of the coloured section, fig. 1, explains this rise of the waters. If this be the case, and that saline waters are continually flowing upon the inclined surfaces of these beds, we can readily explain why they occasionally rise to the surface; for waters collected in the new red sand-stone at higher levels than the surface of the vale of Gloucester, would naturally ascend to their original level by any cracks or open veins which might present themselves in the overlying lias.

The salt water having to pass through various strata of marl and clay, loaded with iron pyrites, or sulphuret of iron, it is to be presumed that during this passage certain chemical changes take place, which give to the waters their most valuable medicinal qualities. The most important process in this moist subterranean laboratory, would be the decomposition of the sulphuret of iron, which supplies a large quantity of sulphate of the oxide of iron, a process which must be highly accelerated by the structure of these incoherent and finely laminated beds, through which the pyrites is so very widely disseminated. The sulphuric acid, thus generated, will necessarily re-act on the different bases, such as magnesia and lime, which it may meet with in the strata, and form those sulphates so prevalent in the higher or pyritous beds of the lias, the oxide of iron being at the same time more or less completely separated. By such means, it is presumed that these Mineral Waters, which are principally brine springs at the greatest depths, acquire additional and valuable properties in their rise. In suggesting this explanation, we must not, however, overlook the fact, that fresh water is perpetually falling from the atmosphere upon the surface of the lias clay, more or less percolating its uppermost strata. Many of the saline springs must therefore be somewhat affected by this cause, and the existing condition of the various wells of Cheltenham may ultimately depend upon three causes:—

1. The supply of salt water from the inferior new red sand-stone, in the manner above described.

2. The chemical action produced during the filtration of water through the variously constituted strata.

3. The supply of fresh water from the atmosphere.

The chemical relations and medicinal virtues of these celebrated waters have been well described in other treatises, and they have only been mentioned in this place to convey a clear notion of their origin, and their connection with the geological structure of the district."

All writers before Mr. Murchison, considered that the mineral properties of the Cheltenham springs were the consequence of chemical action, supposed to take place during the passage of the waters through beds of magnesian lime-stone lying at the base of the blue clay,—*the lias,*—and the presence, in the latter, of iron pyrites and marine animal remains, impregnating them, as they rose towards the surface, with carbonate of iron and muriate of soda. These guesses at truth were, however, made long prior to the admission of Geology into " the list of the inductive sciences," and ere any of its important discoveries had given it a title to be so.

CHAPTER III.

MINERAL WATERS.

Medicinal Properties of the Saline, Sulphureous, and Chalybeate Waters.

WE have seen, in the last chapter, how geologists and chemists attempt to account for the origin of those mineral impregnations, the presence of which in the Waters of Cheltenham has caused them to become so universally esteemed. What the precise *chemical* nature of those impregnations are, we shall have to explain hereafter, when we come to speak of their analysed contents. At present we shall confine our observations to their medicinal properties merely.

On this subject there have been innumerable treatises published, of which the most celebrated, among the earlier ones, were those of Dr. Short and Dr. Fothergill, who gave to the world the results of their observations and experience in the years 1740, 1788, respectively; and, within the present century, Dr. Jameson, Dr. Scudamore, Dr. Mc Cabe, and Dr. Gibney; and several other members of the faculty have also published their views and opinions on the medical properties and uses of the different Waters. But the most recent Work on the subject is a small treatise, entitled—*The Cheltenham Waters, their nature and properties, with general directions for their use, and brief notices of the diseases in which they are found beneficial, by a Resident Physician.* From this pamphlet we shall make a few extracts, as better adapted for affording satisfactory information to the stranger than any non-medical notices we could substitute.

" The Mineral Waters of Cheltenham may, with propriety, be divided into three classes, viz., the *saline,* the *sulphureous,* and the *chalybeate.* Of these classes there are some varieties, differing only in the *proportions* of their contents, and which are indicated at the spas by different numbers, 1, 2, 3, &c."

" THE SALINE WATERS.—Although all the different Waters of Cheltenham may be said to be *saline,* from their all containing the neutral salts in greater or less proportions; yet it is to those in which these salts predominate and give the medical character to the Water, that we particularly apply the epithet *saline.* These salts give them their leading character, and are easily discovered by their taste, and by their operation on the human body. The principal of these salts are, muriate of soda, sulphate of soda, and sulphate of magnesia; for although, as has been seen by the analysis, other salts are contained in them, it is to these three that they principally owe their medical virtues. The purest salines are the two Nos. 4 at the Montpellier Spa, Nos. 1 and 4 at the Old Wells, and the salines at Pittville and Cambray; and accordingly these are the Waters most frequently drank in all ordinary disorders of the liver, stomach and bowels; in dyspeptic and bilious disorders, nephritic and dropsical affections, female complaints, &c. &c., and many cases of gout and rheumatism. The effects of these Waters are not confined to the secretions of the *bowels;* they act more or less in *all* the secretions, and particularly upon the kidneys and skin;

and thus a continuance in their use for a proper length of time frequently produces a completely altered state of system, and restores healthy function to organs that have long been morbidly affected."

"THE SULPHUREOUS WATERS.—The principal sulphureous springs are Nos. 2 and 3 at the Montpellier Spa, Nos. 2 and 5 at the Old Wells, and the sulphuretted saline at Pittville. We consider that these Waters are very little if any thing inferior in their medical effects to those of Harrowgate; more especially No. 2 at the Montpellier, and No. 5 at the Old Well; several striking instances of benefit derived from their use in long continued and obstinate cutaneous affections, old sores, and ulcer, having come under the observation of the Author. Many persons have been inclined to doubt their efficacy, from the circumstance of their saline ingredients depriving them of the strong sulphureous taste and smell possessed by the waters of Harrowgate; but this is a mistake which experience will correct, and to all those afflicted by cutaneous diseases, scrofula in its various forms, ulcers, rheumatism, gout, hemorrhoids, worms, &c., and many female complaints, we can confidently recommend these Waters as a very valuable remedy, when taken as directed under the several heads of these diseases; in many cases they will affect a complete cure, and in almost all they will afford sensible relief. They do not act particularly upon the stomach or bowels, or at least it is in a very gentle manner; but they act very sensibly on the skin, kidneys, and lungs."

" THE CHALYBEATE WATERS.—These Waters are not inferior in efficacy, in those cases to which they are adapted, to either of the others. In those diseases of debility, with languid circulation and torpid action of the whole system, in which tonics and chalybeates are indicated, they will be found inferior to none in the kingdom; not even to those of Tunbridge Wells. In female complaints especially they are of infinite service in restoring suspended or perverted function, and in generally strengthening the system. In most of the forms of scrofula they are highly valuable; and, in many instances, in convalescence from diseases which have left great debility, a course of these Waters is extremely useful; and in many cases they are indicated after one or two courses of the saline or sulphureous Waters; but in proportion as the chalybeate Waters are beneficial in those cases to which they are adapted, so are they prejudicial if improperly and incautiously taken, and may produce the very worst effects. They never should be had recourse to but under medical advice, as it is impossible for any other than a medical man to judge in what cases and constitutions they may be useful or prejudicial. As a general remark it may be observed, that they seldom or ever agree with persons of active circulation, florid complexion, and sanguine temperament; or persons subject to cough, spitting of blood, determination of blood to the head, &c.; but are well adapted to cold and phlegmatic habits, where there is languid circulation, torpor of the system, &c.; whenever they produce headache, flushings of the countenance, giddiness, &c., their use should be immediately discontinued. The strongest chalybeates at Cheltenham are those of the Cambray Spa, and at the Montpellier Laboratory; and are therefore best adapted for cases in which the use of steel medicines are clearly indicated, and female complaints attended by great debility, scrofula, those cases of dyspepsia in which tonics are indicated, many nervous affections, convalescence from diseases, &c."

Long experience has proved that spring and autumn

are the best seasons for drinking the aperient Waters of
Cheltenham; it is not indeed unusual, should the weather
prove tolerably open, to find, even so early as March, a
great number of invalid visitors assembled at the different
spas in order to seize the earliest possible chances of recovery. From April to August the attendance becomes
daily more numerous. August, September, and October,
are considered as comprehending the height of the season.
The Waters are found to be most effective in their operations when taken early in the morning, and upon an empty
stomach; a practice now so well understood and followed,
that they are seldom or ever drank after ten o'clock. The
usual dose is two or three eight-ounce glasses, taken at
intervals of ten or fifteen minutes between each glass,
moderate exercise being used the while. So various, however, are the constitutions of men, that no absolute rules
can be laid down either for time or quantity. It is to the
general practice only that our remarks must be considered
as applying; the exceptions being necessarily numerous
from the diversity and often discordant complaints incident
to the human frame; a conviction which deters us from
entering into the details of instructions which might, peradventure, if followed indiscriminately, not unfrequently'
do harm where good was intended. In all cases of serious
illness, therefore, we should strongly recommend the patient to have recourse at once to proper medical advice;
which alone can direct him aright in the choice of that particular Water, and the plan to be followed in taking it, that
may be most serviceable to the complaint with which he
may be afflicted.

Numberless persons visit Cheltenham who drink the
Waters during the period of their sojourn, influenced wholly
by the force of example, and without having any other ob-

ject in view, or standing in need of them as medicine. Such invalids should have recourse to the pure saline Water, No. 4, which is less likely, from the peculiarity of its component properties, to prove injurious than some of the others, especially when taken indiscriminately and without proper advice. Hence a much greater demand is occasioned for No. 4 than for either of the other numbers; so great, indeed, is this during the summer season that many persons have been led to imagine, without at all enquiring into the matter, that nature alone could not yield water enough to supply the demand for this particular number, and that art is occasionally called in to her aid. An opinion strengthened perhaps by the statements of former Guides, that the wells, Nos. 4 and 5, at the Montpellier Spa, only yielded twenty-four gallons of water daily. As we know this statement has not unfrequently given rise to a misconception in the minds of strangers, it may not be amiss, in explanation thereof, to inform the visitor that the pipe which communicates with the pump in the Rotunda is connected with six or seven wells, all possessing a water of exactly similar properties, and flowing in great abundance into the main well, which is situated a little to the south of the pump-room, and covered over with a neat stone turret. This, as well as all the other wells, both at the Montpellier and at the other spas, are at all times open to public inspection on application to the pumper; but, as the descent is somewhat dark and perilous, very few persons have troubled themselves to examine their deep and subterraneous issues.

The Waters being too cold for many delicate stomachs, arrangements exist at all the Spas for warming them, to obviate the medical objections urged against their administration in their natural state; and though frequently taken as drawn from the well, most persons seem now to prefer them of a lukewarm temperature. A solution of the Cheltenham Salts is occasionally added by the pumpers, when the Waters themselves are not found sufficiently active. But this is not done except when specially desired, either by the patient or his medical adviser.

It should be ever borne in mind by those who visit Cheltenham for the purposes of health, and, consequently, desire to derive benefit from the use of its Mineral Waters, that these are at all times most effective when drunk at the fountain head: the habit, therefore, not unfrequently indulged in, of drinking them at home, is much to be deprecated, as, however carefully conveyed, it is impossible but that their delicate gaseous contents must be dissipated by the process of bottling, added to which it generally happens that exercise is, under such circumstances, wholly foregone; and this, it is well known, is a powerful auxiliary to the healthful operations of the Waters themselves. It is advisable also to discontinue their use gradually; and where the drinker is unable, from circumstances, to observe this practice, he should provide himself with some of the real Cheltenham Salts, which he can take occasionally at his own home, and which will be found the best possible substitute for the Spa Waters.

CHAP. IV.

THE SPAS AND PUMP ROOMS.

Discovery of the Waters—The Old Wells—Montpellier Spas—Present Analysis—Pittville—Cambray Saline and Chalybeate Spa—Other Mineral Waters.

HAVING in the two chapters immediately foregoing, given a minute description of all the different Mineral Waters which the soil of Cheltenham produces, and also of their peculiar medical properties, it is our purpose now to conduct the stranger to the several establishments whence those Waters are dispensed to the public, and to initiate him into the mysteries of the Pump Room. The various Spas constitute the lions of the place, and it behoves, therefore, that we give a " full, true, and particular account" of each.—To begin then with the beginning.

Upwards of a century has now gone by since the sanative virtues of the Cheltenham Waters were first noticed, and probably another century might have elapsed ere the discovery had taken place, but for the following simple incident, preserved by tradition, and, for lack of a better, now generally received as accredited history.

In a meadow, situated at the foot of Bay's Hill, and belonging at the time in question (1716) to Mr. Mason, a small rivulet that silently oozed from the earth, was observed to attract the neighbouring pigeons, great numbers of which generally congregated round the spot, exhibiting a marked predilection for that particular water. Curiosity being awakened by the circumstance, it was observed that in the depth of winter this brooklet continued to flow when other and much larger streams were frozen. The spring being examined, was found to contain a strong saline impregnation, and having been subsequently submitted to experiment, the result proved the medicinal properties of the water to be such as entitled it to take precedence of every other known mineral water in the kingdom.

In allusion to the above legend, the figure of a pigeon is still retained as the crest and cognizance of the

OLD WELLS,

and serves as a pretty ornament to its gates and enclosures, arresting the attention of the inquisitive stranger, and reminding the resident of the humble origin of his much favoured town, now acknowledged to be without a rival among even the fairest of the cities of Europe.

At the time of these first discoveries, the land, as just stated, belonged to a Mr. Mason, who, in 1718, enclosed the spring and erected a small shed over its issue. Considerable benefit having been derived from drinking the Waters, the proprietor submitted them in 1721 to the analytical experiments of Drs. Baird and Greville, whose opinions coincided with those of the several other medical men, who had already pronounced them to be of a very superior description. Thus sanctioned, the Waters were now, for the first time, regularly sold as a medicine, the Spa being let to a Mr. Spencer, who took a lease of the property at the annual rental of sixty-one pounds.

On the death of Mr. Mason and his son, the Old Wells and the Bays Hill estate came into the possession of Capt.

H. Skillicorne, the husband of Mr. Mason's daughter, who resolved to turn the then recent discoveries to a more profitable account. He, accordingly, in the summer of 1738, built rooms on the western side of the walk for the reception and accommodation of the company frequenting the spa, and raised a small dome on four brick arches as a protection to the well, which was at the same time deepened to nine feet below the surface, and covered with a wooden trap door—a stone reservoir being placed beneath the pump in which to collect and preserve the Water. In consequence of these additions and improvements, and the better regulated system of arrangements which was simultaneously adopted, the year 1738 became to be considered as the date of the establishment of the Old Wells, which were now honoured with the appellation of the *Cheltenham Spa*. Capt. Skillicorne likewise formed the Grand Walk or Parade, as it was then called, and converted the adjacent meadows into pleasure grounds and gardens; in 1743 planting the avenue of elms, now forming the principal walk, which was originally intended by Lord Bottetourt, who is said to have been the author of the design, to have extended to the church, but this intention was frustrated, by the owners of the intervening land refusing to entertain the propositions made to them for that purpose; and it was, accordingly, not continued beyond the brook, over which a light bridge connected the "parade" with the public thoroughfare through Church Mead.* This walk measures upwards of three hundred yards in length, by eight in breadth; and is generally admitted to be one of the noblest of its kind in England, rivaling in grandeur many of the most celebrated collegiate and baronial vistas of our land, though necessarily giving rise to trains of thought and

* See before, p. 7.

association widely different. A cottage, built some half a century ago by a Rev. Dr. Walker, and called Grove Cottage, still exists, forming a peculiarly picturesque object at the upper extremity of the walk. It is from the front bow window of this cottage that the finest view of the walk is to be obtained, looking through its entire length

towards St. Mary's church, the spire of which, rising in the distance high above the intervening trees, forms a beautiful and striking termination to the bold and lofty vista; the pump room and contiguous buildings midway down, breaking the continuity of the line of vision, and admitting, through the opening, a broad mass of light into the scene, greatly to the improvement of its general effect. The walk itself is well gravelled, and always kept in very neat order; & within late years a variety of flower beds have been introduced on either side, thereby very

THE OLD WELL WALK.

materially contributing to relieve the sombre feeling which it is almost impossible wholly to separate from scenes of the kind.

As the reputation and celebrity of the Waters increased, the buildings erected in 1738 were soon found inadequate to the accommodation of the annually increasing numbers of the visitors, and, consequently, in 1775, a new pump room, measuring sixty-six feet long by twenty-three wide, was added on the east side of the walk—the premises formerly erected by Capt. Skillicorne being converted into private dwellings. Here, for many years, the principal amusements of Cheltenham centred—music, dancing, card playing, and other kindred diversions being carried on in daily succession; varied occasionally by public breakfasts and evening promenades throughout the season. These gaieties recommended the place to the good opinion and favour of those in quest of pleasure, as much as the medicinal properties of its springs did to the attention of the invalid; and many resorted to it whose only motives for a visit to Cheltenham were the enjoyment of good society and pleasant pastime.

The visit of King George III. and the royal family, in 1788, of which an account has been already given,* brought the Cheltenham Spa so much into fashion, and caused so sudden a run upon its Waters, that the supply often proved inadequate to the demand—the well being, not unfrequently, exhausted of its contents before nine o'clock in the morning. At this time the spring only yielded about 105 gallons per day, and the utmost frugality was, consequently, obliged to be observed, in order that the company might not be disappointed of their morning draughts. This insufficiency formed the subject of frequent and serious deliberations with the writers and authorities of the day; among others both Dr. Fothergill and Dr. Smith offer many suggestions for a more economical system of dispensing the Waters. The latter, who was Savilian professor of geometry at Oxford, and who

* See before—p. 12.

published a treatise on the Waters in 1786, gravely recom-
mends that "seeing the inhabitants have all the Waters
to themselves for seven months of the year" they "should
be a little more sparing of their draughts during the height
of the season, out of respect to those who come from a
distance."* The scarcity of water here adverted to was,
however, shortly remedied by the sinking of fresh wells to
which that sunk by order of George the Third, and called
the King's Well, led the way, affording for some years an
abundant supply.

But these wells were sunk much deeper into the lias
than the original old one, scarcely any medicinal water
making its appearance until the borings had gone down
between thirty and forty feet, at which depths the percola-
tions generally became plentiful as well as strongly impregnated with saline, becoming still more so as the wells
were deepened. The character of the Waters frequently
undergoing important changes, corresponding to the rela-
tive positions of the strata whence they were given.

For the space of full quarter of a century from the date
last named the Old Wells rejoiced in its noontide of prosperity: its most golden recollections are, therefore, associated with the history of this period. The maturing
beauty of its noble walk, thronged, during the season, with
the wealthiest and most distinguished members of the
British aristocracy: its musical entertainments—its authorized assumption of the prefix *Royal*, and, above all, the
reputation of its Waters, united to render it the favourite
spa of England. Shortly after 1812, however, a " change
came o'er the spirit of its dream," and the tide of fashion
and of public favour began slowly to retire from its former
channel, and to flow into that of the Montpellier, now

* *Observations on the Use and Abuse of the Cheltenham Waters*, 1786—p. 16.

putting forth its claims to approbation and support, with a vigour that startled the speculators of the old regeme.

An engraving published about this time, and from which the annexed vignette is copied, affords a view of the Royal Old Wells in their days of greatest prosperity.

THE ROYAL OLD WELLS, 1812.

In the centre of the walk is the arched building, erected by Capt. Skillicorne, in the year 1738, & beneath which the waters continued still to be dispensed, and on the right are the buildings once used as dancing, card, and billiard rooms, but converted into private dwelling houses on the erection of the larger room, on the opposite side of the walk, in 1775: this—now the pump room of the Royal Old Wells—having superseded the arched building formerly covering the principal well, and whence the Waters were of old " retailed " to the public, but which, having fallen into a state of dilapidation and decay, was, in 1837, removed, that the view and thoroughfare of the walk might be open and unimpeded.

From 1812 the attractions of the Royal Old Wells continued year after year to wane before the superior pretensions of its more powerful rival, which, for the last thirty years, has, in a great measure, superseded it in the estimation of the visitors of Cheltenham. But the original spa is still patronized by many families of high distinction; and its Waters, particularly its Sulphur Water, continue to be as strongly recommended by the faculty as ever. On the 8th of August, in the year 1838, the com-

pletion of the centenary of its establishment was celebrated
by a public fête upon a grand and extensive scale; the
town generally taking a lively interest in the event, and
appointing a committee to sanction and superintend the
amusements catered for the occasion. In the morning
there was a public breakfast, followed by dancings on the
green-sward, and other diversions, with performances of
bands of music, &c. A young sapling oak was also planted
in the ground with processional ceremonies, by the lessee,
Miss Hasell, in the hope that it would grow and flourish,
and tell to future generations of the doings of the first
centenary of the Royal Old Wells. In the evening a
crowd of entertainments—musical, scenic, and pyrotech-
nic—afforded abundant entertainment to the multitudes as-

CENTENARY FETE, 1838.

sembled there;
and the walk
was brilliantly
illuminated, the
upper portion
being formed in-
to an extensive
series of arches,
and that below
the pump room
being festooned
from end to end;
either extrem-
ity having beau-
tiful and appropriate devices in gas. Thousands of spec-
tators thronged the walks and gardens, and a spectacle
was presented such as had never before been witnessed in
Cheltenham. A sketch of the scene was lithographed by
Mr. Rowe, a resident artist, from which the annexed

vignette has been copied. A medal, commemorative of
the event, was struck for the occasion, and the first impression in gold was presented, with a suitable address,
to her Majesty. The anniversary of the centenary fête
continues to be celebrated as a gala day at one or other of
the spas annually in the month of August.

The pump room, built by Messrs. Skillicorne and Miller,
in 1775, has, within late years, been considerably improved,
and approaches formed immediately off the high road, by
which the company frequenting the spa are enabled to
be set down under cover, which formerly was not the
case, greatly to the inconvenience of the carriage invalid,
who was compelled, in all weathers, to walk a considerable
distance to the entrance of the pump room.   In the or-
chards and grounds surrounding the pump room several
ornamental little buildings have been erected, which serve
the double purpose of indicating the sites of the various
wells, and securing them from injury either of weather or
injudicious curiosity.

The Royal Old Wells are at present the property of
a joint stock company, who purchased the Bays Hill estate
from W. N. Skillicorne, Esq., in the year 1838, and by
whom the spa is let on lease to Miss Hasell, its present
tenant, who is ceaseless in her efforts to please the public,
and to merit by every attention to the wants and wishes
of her subscribers that patronage and support awarded to
the establishment in its former palmy days.   During the
season, that is, from May to October, one or two musicians
are generally engaged to perform in the mornings, from
eight to ten o'clock; and not unfrequently there is music
also in the afternoons: and there are occasionally in the
summer evenings exhibitions of fireworks and other enter-

tainments, such as are usually got up at similar establishments, and suited to the open air.

There are now six varieties of Mineral Water at this establishment, which are numbered, and, with the exception of the first, described according to their predominating chemical properties.

No. 1. The Original or Old Wells.	No. 4. Strong Saline.
2. Sulphuretted Saline.	5. Strong Sulphuretted Saline.
3. Strong Chalybeate Saline.	6. Strong Muriatic Saline.

The following are the terms of subscription for drinking the Spa Waters at the pump room of the Royal Old Wells:

A FAMILY.				ONE PERSON.			
For the Season	£2	2	0	For the Season	£1	1	0
Three Months	1	11	6	Three Months ..	0	17	0
One Month....	1	1	0	One Month	0	10	6
A Fortnight ..	0	15	0	A Fortnight ..	0	7	6
A Week	0	10	6	A Week	0	5	0

These payments entitle the subscriber to each of the different kinds of Waters above enumerated, free of any other charge, except that it is usual to present the pumper with some gratuity for her services, at the termination of the period to which the subscription applies. Non-subscribers are charged one shilling per morning.

In addition to the above, persons using the walks connected with this spa, and which are kept in order at considerable cost, are expected to subscribe towards defraying a portion of the expenses incurred thereby. The terms of this subscription are as under:

A Family, for the Season 10s. 6d.		One Person for 3 months 3s. 6d.	
Two Persons	do.	7s. 0d.	A Family for 1 month	5s. 0d.
One Person	do.	5s. 0d.	One Person	2s. 6d.
	A Family for 3 months	7s. 6d.		

Second in the order of time, though first in that of importance, is the

MONTPELLIER SPA,

situate about half a mile southward of the town. The direct road to this establishment forms a line of continuation with the Promenade grand drive, leading from the High Street to the Queen's Hotel, which it leaves on the left, and proceeding through Montpellier Avenue,—a thoroughfare opened some ten or twelve years ago,—passes between the pump room and the gardens in which the principal public amusements connected therewith, are carried on.

From the time when George the Third visited Cheltenham, and public attention became thereby more particularly directed to the sanative virtues of its mineral springs, each succeeding year brought with it an increase of visitors, and the demand upon the wells became, therefore, greater during the season, than they could satisfy; added to which, several of those which had formerly furnished a most abundant supply, now altogether failed. Great inconvenience being caused by this circumstance, the proprietors of lands immediately adjoining the Bays Hill Estate resolved to attempt the discovery of similar Waters upon THEIR property, nor were they disappointed in their anticipations of the results.

Between the years 1800 and 1806 Dr. Jameson was particularly active in endeavouring to discover fresh springs, and succeeded in several instances in obtaining large temporary supplies from borings made at different points around Mr. Skillicorne's land; but most of them became, after a time, exhausted, or underwent such changes as to cause them to be successively deserted and abandoned. The investigations of Dr. Jameson led the way to a more accurate knowledge of the nature and properties of the sub-soil of the neighbourhood, and particularly of the lias formation in which the Mineral Waters were supposed to have their origin, and which it was found extended, in every direction, round the town, at slightly varying depths below the surface—thus accounting for the great profusion of incipient spas which, about this time, started into existence, and two or three of the most promising of which have been already noticed.

But by far the most successful among the experimenters of that day was H. Thompson, Esq., who, in 1806, was fortunate enough to arrive at several very fine mineral springs upon an estate which he had then recently purchased. Having satisfied himself of the medicinal properties of the Waters which he had discovered, he shortly commenced turning his discoveries to a profitable account, erecting a pump room, which, in the summer of 1809, was opened to the public. This, which was the first Montpellier Pump Room, was a neat and summer-like building,

 supported in front and at either end on wooden pillars, forming a sort of veranda, beneath which the company promenaded in bad weather, & above the centre

MONTPELLIER PUMP ROOM, 1809.

of which a small music room or orchestra was built for the accommodation of the band, which performed there every morning during the Water drinking season, and which proved a great attraction to the spa.

Encouraged by the success of his first undertaking, Mr. Thompson continued boring for other springs in order to supply the still constantly increasing demand; and to such an extent did he carry on his experiments in this particular, that at the time of his death, which took place Nov. 2, 1820, he had upwards of EIGHTY different wells upon his estate, all yielding a greater or less proportion of Mineral Waters, and some of them widely different in their chemical properties from any that had been previously known. Several of these wells were sunk in the pump room and immediately around it; but the springs were found to abound most in the land now known as the Lansdowne and Christ Church estates, and the former of which has been since nearly covered with houses— the wells having been domed over as the buildings proceeded, and the pumps, by means of which their contents are procured, being placed at fixed distances with subterranean ways communicating with them. On the Christ

Church estate, which has been more recently planned and laid out for building, several of the original wooden sheds erected over the mouths of the wells, are still remaining; and about midway down the broad road, fronting the church, an old thatched cottage, of a rather picturesque ap-

THE PUMPER'S COTTAGE.

pearance, and at the back of which an odd looking square projection juts out, may, perchance, arrest the stranger's attention, and cause momen-

tary wonder at its continuance in the midst of improvements and alterations so extensive as those which have taken place around it within the last ten years. This rustic habitation is the pumper's cottage, and is occupied by the man who takes charge of the numerous wells which supply the pump room, or, when occasion requires, furnish Waters for the manufacture of the Real Cheltenham Salts, and which being first collected in a large reservoir—the projection above referred to—are thence forced down, by means of pumps through a succession of leaden pipes, to the Laboratory in the Bath Road, a distance of more than a mile.

The discovery of such abundant sources of Mineral Waters soon became extensively known throughout the kingdom, and the influx of company which followed thereupon rendered it necessary, in a very few years, to increase the means of accommodation: additions were annually made to the buildings first erected, and the pump room of 1806 being thought too insignificant for the growing im-

portance of the new spa, Mr. Thompson, in 1817, removed
the veranda'd edifice before described, and on its scite
erected a spacious promenade room, measuring seventy
feet in length and
25 in breadth,
having a neat
and commodious
stone colonnade
in front and at
both ends, sur-
mounted, above
the principal en-
trance, by a lion

MONTPELLIER PUMP ROOM, 1817.

couchant, sculptured in a bold and masterly style. This
architectural re-arrangement brought with it other changes,
and involved many alterations and additions not at first
contemplated, but which were rendered almost inevitable
by time and circumstances. The Band, which then consisted of six instruments, having been dislodged from its
former summer house, and increased in number, was
placed under the north colonnade, in the situation which
it has ever since occupied; and in addition to the regular
morning performances during the time the company attended the spa for the purpose of drinking the Waters,
the practice long existing at the Royal Old Wells, of performing also occasionally on fine evenings during the season, was about the same time introduced, thus leading the
way to the establishment of those Musical Promenades
which have since become the favourite and the most
characteristic of all the amusements of Cheltenham. Con-
temporaneously with the enlargement of the pump room
the capabilities of the Montpellier property were further
developed by its enterprising and skilful proprietor.

But by far the most important of all the improvements
and alterations which the Montpellier pump-room has undergone since its first establishment, was that accomplished
in the winter of 1825-6, by Pearson Thompson, Esq., the
son and successor of the original founder.   We allude to
the erection of the present magnificent ROTUNDA, designed

MONTPELLIER ROTUNDA, 1826.

by, and built under the direction of J. B. Papworth, Esq.,
one of the most eminent architects of the day, and which
is acknowledged on all hands to be unrivalled, as a pump-
room, in any part of Europe.   Without rigidly following
any particular style of architecture, the internal arrangements of the building present nothing that can offend the
most refined and cultivated taste.   The ornaments are extremely chaste, and especially the panelling of the dome;

and the rich marble counters and chimney-pieces, though apparent excrescences to the building, are yet in the most perfect keeping with the general tone of decoration observed throughout. The portions below the dome are beautifully papered in imitation of marbles and scagliolas, which impart a sense of agreeable coolness to the feeling, on entering the apartment, from the hot sunshine of a summer's day. The pump case is surmounted by a finely executed model of the famous Warwick vase, a work of art which the visitor would do well not to let pass unnoticed. On either side of the Rotunda, opening with large glass doors, was formerly a conservatory, regularly furnished with an abundant supply of the choicest exotics, and which, reflected as these were in the large mirrors placed round the room, gave an appearance of truly Arcadian beauty to the whole interior; but these elegant accompaniments have lately been removed, and the apartments converted into billiard rooms. On one side of the Rotunda is a card room appropriated to the use of the subscribers to the summer balls, and on the opposite side the large room occupied as a reading room, and forming a part of the Montpellier Library, an establishment of which we shall have occasion to speak more at large in another place. The diameter of the Rotunda is fifty feet; and its height, to the apex of the lantern which surmounts the dome, fifty-four feet.

The Waters of the Montpellier Spas are of six different kinds, and are named and numbered in the following order:

No. 1.	Chalybeate Saline.	No. 4.A.	Ioduretted Saline.
No. 2.	Strong Sulphurated Saline.	No. 5.	Chalybeated Magnesian
No. 3.	Weak Sulphurated Saline.		Saline.
No. 4.	Pure Saline.	No. 6.	Muriated Saline.

The foregoing comprehend every kind of Mineral Water, except the pure chalybeates, which the soil of Cheltenham has hitherto been known to produce, while Nos. 4 and 5 are peculiar to this establishment; for though Waters similar, in many respects, to these, exist at all the other spas, they are found to differ materially in their chemical properties; a circumstance, we believe, mainly to be ascribed to the different depths of the wells whence the Waters are, in the first instance, drawn. Those which yield the pure saline at the Montpellier do not exceed in depth fifty feet, whereas those which produce the saline Waters at the other spas are from eighty to a hundred feet; and it is generally found that, in proportion as the wells are deepened, the waters acquire a more abundant impregnation of muriate of soda, or common sea salt, which communicates to them a stronger briny taste, without however adding to their medicinal virtues.

These Waters have been analysed at different times by some of the ablest chemists of our country, particularly by Sir Humphrey Davy, Mr. Accum, and Messrs. Brande and Parke; the results of the experiments performed by the last two gentlemen (and published in the 5th No. of the Journal of the Royal Institution) were, for many years, received as the most correct. But, in 1832, Mr. J. T. Cooper having been at great labour in examining afresh the Waters of the Montpellier Spas, the results of his analysis are now, as the most recent, generally adopted. As it may not be uninteresting to many of our readers to be further informed respecting the history of this analysis, we here present them with a short account, extracted from the 1st vol. of the *Cheltenham Looker-On.*

" In the Autumn of 1832, the ingenious chemist above named, being in Cheltenham, was consulted by Messrs.

Jearrads, the then proprietors of the Montpellier Spas, as to the correctness of the analysis made of the Waters by Messrs. Brande and Parke. A very few experiments upon one or two of them soon convinced him that either the analysis in question had been, in the first instance, incorrect, or (what was more probable) that the Waters themselves had undergone a material change since the latter gentlemen made their observations.

" In the inquiry now about to be entered upon, in consequence of this discovery, Mr. Cooper's first attention was directed to the obtaining accurate returns of the gaseous contents of each Water; and in order to effect this, so as to remove all doubts as to the correctness of the results at which he might arrive, his experiments were performed upon Waters drawn immediately from the wells, and not pumped up by the usual process. The results thus obtained were then checked by a series of like experiments upon the Waters at the pump room, and which produced precisely similar results—results, indeed, so similar as to satisfy Mr. Cooper that none of the essential gases were ever dissipated by the process of conveying the Waters from the springs to the pump room.

" Having ascertained the respective proportions of the more ethereal contents of the Spa Waters, as above stated, the next point to be determined was their solid contents; and in order to do this effectually, Mr. Cooper took with him to London a quantity of each Water drawn from the wells, and during last winter* pursued his experiments upon them for the purpose just stated. This was necessarily a long and tedious process, as the employment of the most delicate tests was required, as well as the greatest care in their application. Every difficulty, however, was

* The winter of 1832-3.

surmounted, and the results obtained were in the highest degree satisfactory. We should observe that, in order to place the correctness of the analysis made in London upon small quantities of the Water beyond all doubt, they were checked and compared with the results of ten gallons of each, evaporated at a low temperature, at the Laboratory in Cheltenham. The evidence thus obtained by the latter process, confirmed in every particular the correctness of the London analysis."

" *Contents of the Montpellier Spa Waters, taken from their respective Wells, and analysed by J. T. Cooper, Esq.*

" The quantity of each Water subjected to analysis for the determination of the Saline contents was ten gallons.

No. 1.—*Saline Chalybeate.*

Specific Gravity, 1.005.

Gaseous contents in a Pint,

Carbonic acid	2.5 cub. in.

Saline contents,

Sulphate of Soda	14.7
——— of Lime	1.3
——— of Magnesia	4.0
Muriate of Soda	27.0
Bi-Carbonate of Soda	1.1
Oxide of Iron	.3
	48.4

" This Water also contains an inappreciable quantity of ' Hydrobromate ' of Soda, as also a very minute portion of ' Hydriodate of Soda, but quantities esteemed as hardly worth regarding; and the same may be said of any other substances where the word ' trace ' occurs.

" No. 2.—*Sulphuretted Saline.*

Specific Gravity, 1.008.

Gaseous contents in a Pint,

Sulphuretted Hydr.	1.6 cub. in.
Carbonic Acid	.4

Saline contents,

Muriate of Soda	35.3
Sulphate of Soda	28.4
——— of Magnesia	7.2
——— of Lime	3.1
Oxide of Iron	.42
Hydriodate of Soda	.15
	74.57

" No. 3.—*Weak Sulphuretted Saline.*

Specific Gravity, 1.007.

Gaseous contents in a Pint,

Sulphuretted Hydr.	0.7 cub. in.
Carbonic Acid	0.4

Saline contents,

Muriate of Soda	32.3
Sulphate of Soda	26.5
——— of Magnesia	6.1
——— of Lime	3.3
Oxide of Iron	.41
Hydriodate of Soda	.15
	68.76

" No. 4.—*Pure Saline.*

Specific Gravity, 1.039.

Gaseous contents in a Pint,

Carbonic Acid	1.4 cub. in.

Saline contents,

Muriate of Soda	52.4
Sulphate of Magnesia	14.2
——— of Soda	17.2
Bi-Carbonate of Soda	1.2
Sulphate of Lime	2.7
Hydriodate of Soda, & Hydro-bromate of Soda	a trace.
Carbonate of Lime, and Carbonate of Magnesia ..	1.1
	88.8

F

" No. 4, A.—*Ioduretted Saline.*

Specific Gravity, 1.0101.

Gaseous contents in a Pint,

    Carbonic Acid .... 1.6. cub. in.

    Sulphuretted Hydrogen, a trace.

Saline contents,

Muriate of Soda	51.4
——— of Lime	8.3
——— of Magnesia	7.5
Sulphate of Soda	14.0
——— of Magnesia	17.1
Sulphate of Lime	2.1
Bi-Carbonate of Soda	2.4
Carbonate of Lime, and Carbonate of Magnesia	3.2
Hydriodate of Soda	.25
	106.25

This Water (No. 4, A.) was never before analysed.

" No. 5.—*Chalybeated Magnesian Saline.*

Specific Gravity, 1.009.

Gaseous contents in a Pint,

    Carbonic Acid .... 1.2 cub. in.

Saline contents,

Sulphate of Magnesia	47.0
——— of Lime	3.1
Muriate of Magnesia	10.5
——— of Lime	13.1
——— of Soda	9.7
Bi-Carbonate of Soda	1.7
Oxide of Iron	.4
Hydriodate of Soda, with a very small quantity of	
Hydro-bromate of Soda	.35
	85.85

" No. 6.—*Muriated Saline.*

Specific Gravity, 1.009.

Gaseous contents in a Pint,

    Carbonic Acid .... 0.7 cub. in.

Saline contents,

Muriate of Soda	58.7
——— of Lime	9.3
——— of Magnesia	4.5
Sulphate of Lime	2.0
——— of Soda	12.3
Bi-Carbonate of Soda	1.8
Hydriodate of Soda	.2
Carbonate of Magnesia	a trace.
	88.8

" Chalybeate at the Laboratory.

Specific Gravity, 1.0044.

Gaseous contents,

Sulphurated Hydrogen	0.45
Carbonic Acid	0.35

Saline Contents,

Muriate of Soda	41.21
Sulphate of Soda	3.18
Muriate of Lime	1.00
Oxide of Iron	0.35
Bi-Carbonate of Soda	0.27
Hydrodate of Soda, and Hydro-bromate of Soda....	a trace
Carbonate of Lime	a trace
	47.01

" The difference between this Chalybeate and those which are generally met with, consists in its holding in solution with the oxide of iron a quantity of saline matter. The sulphuretted hydrogen ensures that oxide of iron to be in the minimum state of oxidation."

The terms of subscription to the Montpellier Spa Waters are as follows:

	£	s.	d.
A family, for the season	2	2	0
Two persons of the same family, ditto	1	11	6
One person, ditto	1	1	0
One person, for a fortnight	0	10	6

Strangers, and persons who only drink the Waters occasionally, and who do not, therefore, wish to subscribe, are charged a shilling each morning. It is customary to take two glasses, allowing an interval of fifteen minutes between each. In event of the Water in its natural state being too weak to produce the effect desired, which is not unfrequently the case with strong constitutions, the person who serves it can always increase its strength by a solution of the salts, which are themselves produced from these same Waters. As the remuneration of the female pumpers depend entirely upon the voluntary subscriptions of the Water drinkers, it is customary to present them with a gratuity, varying in amount from half-a-crown to half-a-guinea, according to the length of time, or the number of persons of the same family, who may have been in the habit of drinking. The pumper's book, in which such sums are usually entered, is generally placed on the desk, with the other subscription books of the establishment.

The pump room is always open at six o'clock in the morning throughout the year; and, during the height of the season, even at this early hour, many persons are found waiting to partake of the health-restoring stream. It is not, however, until eight o'clock that the major part of the visitors arrive; from that hour to ten the walk and rooms are usually crowded, and a band of seventeen musicians are stationed at the end of the grand promenade, who perform a variety of the most esteemed compositions, as well ancient as modern. Very great attention has been bestowed upon the musical department of this establishment—the performers are selected from London, Bath, and other parts of the country—and the band is acknowledged, by the most competent judges, to be equal to any military band in the kingdom. The leader is at all times willing to have played such compositions as the subscribers may express a desire to hear.

The duration of the season is the same here as at the Royal Old Wells, extending from the beginning of May to the end of October, when the full band is dismissed, and a smaller one, consisting of three or four instruments only, is substituted, performing in the promenade room for some weeks longer. Of late years a manifest alteration has taken place in respect to the fullness or otherwise of the season: formerly it was the custom for strangers to throng to Cheltenham very early in April, and May was generally considered the best month of the twelve; but since the fashion of devoting the spring to the gaieties of London has become universal, our town does not receive any large influx of visitors until summer is far advanced—July, August, and September, with the first fortnight of October, being fullest of company. Those who visit the place for health sake, and whose sole object is to derive benefit from drinking the Spa Waters, still constitute a large proportion of the spring population of the place.

There are few scenes more animated and inspiring than the Montpellier promenade, on a fine summer morning, between eight and ten o'clock. The presence of the lovely, the titled, and the fashionable, as they parade up and down the grand walk to the sound of music, and breathing an atmosphere of sunshine and health, present a scene of living loveliness, unsurpassed by the brightest idealizations of Stothard, or the fairy elysiums of a Spenser; for here indeed it may truly be said, that " ladies' eyes rain influence." The gay scene must be witnessed to be rightly conceived; for nothing can exceed the animation and splendour of the morning promenade, except, indeed, it be that of the evening, of which we shall have more fitting opportunity to speak when particularizing the amusements of the place generally.

The walks, rides, and drives, connected with the Montpellier Spa, are of considerable extent, reaching from the pump room to the Bath road in one direction, and to the salts manufactory in the other. As a great annual expenditure is required to keep them in order, such persons as contribute to their wear and tear, whether residents or visitors, are expected also to contribute towards the expenses necessarily incurred. The terms of subscription are as follow:

	To the walks. £ s. d.	Walks, rides, and drives. £ s. d.
A family	0 12 0	0 15 0
Two persons of the same family..	0 8 0	0 10 6
One person	0 5 0	0 7 6
Family not exceeding a fortnight	0 5 0	
One Person ditto	0 3 6	

We have thus endeavoured to describe in the leading circumstances connected with the rise, progress, and present state of the Royal Old Wells and the Montpellier Spas, which now divide between them the greater portion of the Water drinking of Cheltenham—advancing their respective claims to public support in a spirit of honourable rivalry. It is true the harmony which generally distinguishes their relationship, experiences occasional interruptions, but these are, fortunately, of short continuance; and whatever little jealousies manifest themselves, they have seldom been known to lead to acts of discourtesy—effects which too often result from ill regulated emulation. Still they are not wholly unobservable, as the following pointed and elegant composition, from the pen of W. H. Merle, Esq., and published some years ago (1835) in the *Cheltenham Looker-On*, will sufficiently evince.

DIALOGUE BETWEEN " THE OLD WELL WALK " AND " THE YOUNG WELL WALK."

I.

Said the Young Well Walk to the Old Well Walk,
   In the pride of her apple bloom,—
" Come and chat with the Belle, come my old ' Mother Well,'
   And desert from your shady gloom.

" By my sweet pretty soul, you may rival King Cole,
   Who once call'd for his fiddlers three,
But his palace was dark, like a coal without spark ;
   Come and bask in the sun with me.

" You may boast, if you please, of your tall maiden trees,
   Which extend in a line to St. Mary's ;
But a maid, be it told, is not valued when old ;
   Come and walk in the land of the fairies."

II.

Said the Old Well Walk to the Young Well Walk,
   In the pride of her numbered years,
" Pretty babe, you are young, and the wisdom of tongue
   Must be learnt in the valley of tears.

Your laburnum and larch, will they e'er form the arch
   Which instructed the genius of man ?*
And your lilac and thorn, tho' in blossom, I scorn,
   Short, indeed, is the length of their span !

" Better come to the grove where the turtles make love,
   And the church is for ever in sight ;
Let the bird tell of hope—and the church be a trope
   Of the joys that shall never take flight."

III.

Said the Young Well Walk to the Old Well Walk,
   As the blood of her bosom boiled up,
" Do you think at my years I will drink of your tears ?—
   No, I'll sip from the honey-dew cup.

" Pretty notions of wooing ! with your doves and their cooing !
   I had rather make love my own self :
Why your sayings and saws, scarce the rooks and jackdaws,
   It is time they were laid on the shelf.

* Nature's avenue is said to have given rise to the Gothic arch.

" I'm too young, my old friend, for the joys without end,
   And prefer new delights daily given;
All your proverbs are lumber, save one of the number,
   Which reminds you who's farthest from heaven."*

IV.

Said the Old Well Walk to the Young Well Walk,
   With a frown of most matronly rage,
" Empty belle! silly lass! like the tinkling of brass
   Are your words to the wisdom of age.

" Will you never grow wise till misfortunes arise,
   And reveal the just measure of worth;
You forget that my form would defy the same storm
   Which would prostrate your beauty to earth.

" You forget what is done by that tanner, the sun,
   To the silks and the skin of fair daughters—
That your gardens, when damp, give the cholic and cramp,
   And undo all the good of your waters!"

V.

The Young Well Walk was about to talk,
   And reply rather pertly, we fear,
When a strong northern gust stopped her mouth with the dust,
   And cut short the young lady's career.

Pealed the thunder along, like the Mexican gong,
   While they carved out a heart for their god;
Beauty, blossom and flower, where o'erwhelmed by a shower,
   And soon borne to the pitiless sod.

When the storm had gone by, the Old Walk looked on high,
   In the strength of her Majesty's pride;
Tho' she held up her head, conscience whispering said,
   " I am cruelly chilled within side."

From that time, I've been told, the Young Walk and the Old
   Without words have divided their reign;
They have not only felt, but have actually dwelt,
   As all neighbours should feel and remain.

---

* " The nearest the church the farthest from heaven."—*Old Proverb.*

Since they spoke not again, we are bound to explain,
   How they brought their disputes to a close:
As is usual, the Old—had the pleasure to scold;
   And the Young—ruled the day as she chose.

Besides the two establishments already so fully described, there is, on the south side of the town, one other,
which demands a passing notice—namely,

THE CAMBRAY CHALYBEATE
AND SALINE SPA,

a neat little gothic pump room opposite the north-east
corner of Imperial Square. This Chalybeate, the spring
of which was first discovered in 1807, was for many
years known as Fowler's Spa, and was dispensed to the
Water drinkers of Cheltenham from a small cottage at the

bottom of Cambray. Its peculiar excellence consists, as may be inferred from its appellation, in the predominance of its chalybeate impregnations. Waters of this description are considered very serviceable in cases of weak and debilitated stomachs, and, in short, in all disorders requiring the use of highly tonic medicines. The analysis of the Cambray spring, made some years ago by Mr. Accum, gave the following as the chemical contents of a wine-gallon of the Water:

Specific Gravity, 1.0011.

	GRAINS.
Carbonate of Iron	7.05
Muriates of Lime and Magnesia	15.50
Muriate and Sulphate of Soda	24.00
Sulphate of Lime	2.00
Carbonate of Magnesia and Lime	8.95
Solid contents	64.50

GASEOUS CONTENTS.
Carbonic Acid Gas, 24 cubic inches.

In addition to the Chalybeate Water, for which this spa has ever been most celebrated, a saline spring was discovered in 1834, immediately beneath the pump room, which was then, and not till then, erected over the well; the chalybeate being conveyed in pipes to the same spot from the garden of Cambray House, the residence of the proprietor, Mr. B. Jones, in which it has its origin. The Saline Water has been analysed by Faraday, and appears to be very similar in its properties to those of the other spas. The well is sixty-six feet deep.

THE ANALYSIS OF MR. FARADAY,
In a Wine Imperial Pint.

Specific Gravity, 1006.7.

	GRAINS.
Muriate of Soda	51.06
Muriate of Lime	8.60
Muriate of Magnesia	a trace.
Sulphate of Soda	17.04
Carbonate of Lime	0.80
Carbonate of Iron	a mere trace.
	77.50

A STRONG CHALYBEATE SPRING, similar in its properties to that of the Cambray Spa, exists at the Cheltenham Salts Manufactory, in the Bath road, and of this, subscribers to the Montpellier Spas have the privilege of drinking, without any extra charge; or persons not subscribing to the Spa Waters at that pump room, may subscribe for this independently, the terms being half-a-guinea each for the course. The analysis of this Water has been already given at page 67.

A third Chalybeate Spa once existed in a meadow to the left of the High Street from the London road, and hard by the mill; but this has been closed now for some years; as has also a saline spring known by the name of the "Alstone Spa," and situated much lower down in the High Street, the direct road to it being through St. George's Place.

———

Having introduced our stranger to the spas and pump rooms situated southward of the High Street, noticing each according to the date and order of its foundation, we must now conduct him to the grand object of attraction on the north side of the town—the last erected as well as the most splendid of all the Water drinking establishments of Cheltenham—

PITTVILLE.

Starting from the Plough Hotel, the visitor will proceed up the street immediately opposite, as thereby he will be conducted in a direct line to this spa, which is distant from the High Street about three quarters of a mile. It is situated upon a considerable eminence, and forms a bold and striking object, as it rises upon the view from the Winchcomb Street approach.

The first stone of this noble edifice was laid, with great parade and ceremony, by the late Joseph Pitt, Esq., the then proprietor, on the 4th of May, 1825. At this time every thing promised fair for its becoming, as was indeed intended, the nucleus of a second town, rivalling its parent Cheltenham both in extent and importance. To this end, one hundred acres of land were marked out for building lots, and these were all bought up with eager avidity by the more speculating inhabitants of the town, even before a stone of the pump room had been laid; and the excited imaginations of the adventurers saw crescents, terraces, and villas, spring up before them, like the enchanted cities of Arabian romance, in the perspective of a very few years. Large fortunes were to be speedily realized, and wealth the sure and certain reward of all who embarked in this new undertaking—this *El Dorado* of the sanguine and the visionary! But scarcely had these golden dreams assumed even a dream-like consistency, when the commercial panic which at this period seized the country, dissolved the magic spell, and the " baseless fabric" of prosperity melted into " thin air;" thus furnishing another practical illustration of the beautiful fable of Alnaschar and his basket of glass. Of the six hundred houses which were to have been immediately erected around Pittville, scarce one hundred made their appearance above the soil during the first ten years. Nothing daunted, however, by the failure of the major part of his co-operators, Mr. Pitt proceeded single-handed to the completion of his portion of the original design. The grounds were all laid out and planted, and the pump room erected, in defiance of every obstacle and discouragement, and at a cost of not less than sixty thousand pounds. The consequence of this spirit of enterprize shown by the principal proprietor was, that year after year, since 1830, many excellent houses were built on the Pitt-ville estate, and down to the present time additions continue to be constantly made to their number, until at length an important and populous neighbourhood has risen up along all the lines of approach to the spa. As several of the rows and terraces already finished will be noticed here-after in our chapter on the streets and public thorough-fares, we shall now proceed at once to speak of the pump room itself, which was built from the designs of Mr. J. Forbes, an architect of Cheltenham.

As seen from the principal approach up the promenade, the Pittville Pump Room presents a bold and imposing front. A noble colonnade, 20 feet wide, formed of Ionic pillars, surrounds three sides of the building. Over the grand entrance is a colossal statue of the goddess Hygeia, and others of Esculapius and Hypocrates, over either wing. Through the centre of the upper story an elegant dome rises to the height of 70 feet from the ground, and a light gallery, into which the entrances of the upper apartments open, runs round its base. The interior of the dome is beautifully ornamented with richly worked panels, having a flower within the square of each, and the same order of elaborate decoration is observed throughout the ceilings of the other parts of the building. The room itself measures 84 feet long by 38 wide, and 34 high.

The pump and counter are placed to the right of a semi-circular recess exactly facing the principal entrance. They are formed of some beautiful specimens of marbles and scagliolas; and here it is that the Spa Waters are served out to the company. The eye of taste is, perhaps, not altogether pleased with the introduction of so showy and glittering a pump case in this situation, as its brilliant and variegated colours appear to harmonize imperfectly with those parts of the interior with which it enters into immediate comparison.

Pittville Pump Room was first opened on Tuesday, July 20th, 1830, upon which occasion a grand public breakfast was given; an entertainment which was repeated on the 21st of August following, in honour of the king's birth day. From this date it takes its rank among the recognised spas of Cheltenham, though its distance from the town very much interferes with its success; as indeed it ever must do, until Fashion, or some other goddess as wayward as Fashion, shall be able to divert the current of patronage from the southern to the northern side of the High Street. Two or three public breakfasts are generally given at Pittville during the season, but no regular series of other amusements have as yet been established. The Pittville Waters consist of a strong and a weak pure saline and a sulphurated saline; the first has been analysed by Drs. Daubeny, Turner, and Daniell. Their experiments, however, gave results differing in some particulars from each other, though they appear, at least those of the first two, to have been performed simultaneously in the spring of 1830. The following is Dr. Daubeny's analysis:

Specific gravity, 1.006.

Solid contents in one pint, 52 grains.

		Grains.
Carbonate of Lime	....	0.20
Sulphate of Lime	....	0.89
Sulphate of Soda	....	17.55
Chloride of Sodium	....	27.16
Magnesia	....	a trace
Bromine	....	.02
Iodine	....	a trace
		45.82

Dr. Turner gave 58.8 as the solid contents of a pint of this Water.

Dr. Daniell's analysis of the weak pure saline, gave 57.2 grains of solid matter to a pint; the contents of which were:—

	Grains.
Sulphuric Acid	7.3
Chlorine	26.6
Sodium	17.7
Soda	3.6
Magnesium	0.7
Lime	1.0
	56.9

The rides, drives, and walks, connected with this establishment, are by far the most extensive of any of those already noticed; and, taken in all their serpentine windings, cover an extent of four or five miles. The garden-grounds are laid out with great taste, and a liberality which seemed to scorn the calculation of expense. In front of the pump room, and at the foot of the grand promenade, is a spacious lake, crossed at either end by a handsome stone bridge. These, though they increase the distance to the pump room, add materially to the picturesque beauty of the surrounding scenery. The visitor of Cheltenham who, during his stay amongst us, shall neglect to take a walk as far as Pittville, must never hope to stand excused in the eye of taste; for, independent of its own intrinsic attractions, the views of the town and neighbourhood, which are obtained from the elevated ground upon which the pump room stands, are such as amply to recompense him for the gentle labour of the ascent. One of the large apartments up stairs has been fitted up as a Cosmorama, in which a series of beautiful and well executed pictorial subjects are exhibited. A separate charge of one shilling is made for

this Cosmoramic exhibition; which charge, however, entitles the party to a view from the outside of the dome--
itself an ample compensation for the additional cost.

The terms of subscription to the Pittville Waters are
nearly the same as at the other spas.

The following are the terms of subscription to the Rides
and Walks: .

	A FAMILY.			FOR ONE PERSON.	
	£	s	d	s	d
For twelve months	1	1	0	15	0
—— three ditto .. ··........	0	15	0	12	6
—— one month	0	10	6	7	6
—— fortnight	0	7	6	5	0

Non-Subscribers are charged 1s. each, or 2s. 6d. for a
family, for admission into the Walks and Pleasure Grounds
beyond the bridges.   For promenading in the Gardens below the bridges no charge is insisted upon, but it is expected, where parties avail themselves of them frequently,
or of the Rides and Drives, that they should become subscribers to the Pump Room Books.

CHAPTER V.

PUBLIC BATHS.

Antiquity of Bathing—Victoria Baths—The Montpellier Baths—Laboratory for the Real Cheltenham Salts—Process of Evaporation—Different kinds of Salts.

THE majority of the persons who visit Cheltenham during the season, do so chiefly with a view of benefiting their health, and their first enquiries, accordingly, have reference directly or indirectly to this important end. Impressed with the conviction that such is the case, we have noticed the Spas and Pump Rooms of the town at some length, assigning them the foremost place in the catalogue of objects of local interest. For the same reason we now proceed to speak of the Baths, bathing being among the most valuable of the remedial agents provided for the alleviation of human suffering, and one which has received the sanction of all civilized nations in all ages of the world. Let it not, however, from this be supposed that we are about to inflict upon the stranger a learned dissertation on the antiquity of the practice, or to demonstrate its advantages by reference to the extraordinary cures which may have been effected through its instrumentality. That there were no baths in existence BEFORE the time of Adam, will, we doubt not, be readily admitted; and that there

G

were few diseases requiring their sanative aid until our Eden-born progenitor partook

" Of that forbidden tree, whose mortal taste
Brought death into our world and all our woes "—

will, perhaps, be deemed equally certain. Without cumbering ourselves, therefore, with any antiquarian researches into the first establishment of public and private baths, or with the effects of warm and cold bathing upon generations of men long since forgotten, we shall proceed at once to consider them in their connection with the living, who will doubtless take more interest in being informed wherein they are themselves most likely to be benefitted by the use of the means in question, than with disquisitions, however learned, upon the baths of the ancient world. But even this does not properly fall within our province, it being rather the duty of the physician than the guide—offices which it shall be our endeavour not to confound; satisfied that we shall most faithfully acquit ourselves in the latter character, when we avoid all interference with the former.

As the celebrity of its Spa Waters increased, and Cheltenham became the general resort of the invalid and the valetudinarian, it was soon found to be the interest of those who had staked large fortunes upon its success, as well as the desire of such as, from more benevolent motives, contributed by their exertions to its permanent establishment, to secure for all who resorted hither, whether in search of pleasure or of health, the advantage of every means likely to secure the chief end which such visitors had in view. Among the most important of these may be ranked the establishment of public baths, comprehending the application of the natural fresh waters of the place, together with such .as might be artificially impregnated to suit the various and varying characters of the diseases seeking to be relieved; and experience has proved that these means, combined with the use of the Spa Waters of Cheltenham, have, in numberless instances, been more conducive to the general restoration and re-establishment of perfect health, than any others which science or art has hitherto discovered.

The first public bath of which any mention is made in Cheltenham, was one called the Cold Bath, which some century ago was built on the Chelt, about two hundred yards from the Old Wells Pump Room; but so far back as 1780 this had fallen into a state of dilapidation and decay, from which it never fully recovered. In the year 1787, however, a Mrs. Freeman established baths, at the London end of the High Street, which, though they have recently passed into other hands, and have changed their name to

THE VICTORIA BATHS,

are still familiarly known by the name of their original founder. Though long since distanced in the race of competition, they continue in the quiet possession of their fair proportion of public patronage and support, and are by no means undeserving even a more liberal share than it has been their good fortune within the last few years to obtain.

Besides the ordinary Warm, Cold, and Shower Baths, procurable at most other similar establishments, the proprietors of the Victoria Baths have recently introduced Whitlaw's apparatus for the application of Medicated Vapour, which has received the sanction and approbation of many of the faculty, and is much recommended for the cure of numerous disorders; but as the indiscriminate or improper use of this invention might be attended with

G 2

injury rather than benefit, recourse should only be had to
it under proper medical advice, or by persons who perfectly understand its principle.

TERMS FOR BATHING.

	s.	d.
Warm or Cold Shower Bath	1	6
Warm Fresh Water ditto	2	0
Warm Salt Water ditto	3	0
Sulphur ditto	3	0
Vapour ditto	4	0
Whitlaw's Patent Medicated Vapour ditto	5	0

Observing the chronological order which we have
hitherto followed, we come now to speak of

THE MONTPELLIER BATHS,

which are situated in the Bath road, adjoining the laboratory for the real Cheltenham Salts, and but a few minutes'
walk from the High Street, through Cambray. This extensive range of buildings was erected by the late Henry
Thompson, Esq., and was considerably enlarged by his
son, Pearson Thompson, Esq. It has also undergone
some very important improvements, especially in its internal arrangements. Originally there were but six baths
in the establishment, two cold, and the other four hot
and tepid. At present, however, there are twenty-five,
comprehending every variety of warm, cold, and shower
baths, douch, and shampooing, as well as the most recent
inventions for the application of hot air and steam.

The WARM BATHS are fourteen in number, one of
these being much larger than the others, and measuring
fourteen feet long by ten broad, and four and a half feet
deep. The process by which the water is heated for these
baths is such as to ensure an uniform and most abundant
supply. A stream of pure spring water which rises at the

back of the premises is conducted underneath the floor of the laboratory, where it comes in contact with a column of steam generated in the spa water boiler, and which has the effect of immediately raising the temperature of the water to an average of 180 degrees of Farenheit. Thus heated, the water flows off in a continued stream into large reservoirs prepared for its reception below the adjoining floors, and thence, as occasion requires, into the different baths, which by this means can be prepared at a minute's notice, and raised to any degree of temperature desired. In the large bath, however, it is in a state of perpetual flow, running constantly in at one end and out at the opposite. The baths themselves are all beautifully lined with marble or white Dutch tile; and the rooms in which they are placed are fitted up with a studied attention to the wants and general convenience of the visitors, amounting indeed to luxury. The apartments are all lighted and ventilated from above, and upon such a plan as to secure a pure and healthy state of atmosphere, while at the same time it renders it impossible for them to be overlooked. Any of these (except the large one) can be used either as fresh water or mineral baths, according to the wishes and instructions of the bather. Impregnations of sulphur or saline are those most commonly in demand.

COLD BATHS.—Any of the small warm baths above described may be employed also for cold bathing; but the principal cold bath of this establishment is one that measures twenty feet long by ten broad and four and a half feet deep. The water here is in constant motion and observes an uniform flow in and out of the bath. It is of a particularly fine quality, and appears as fresh and pellucid as if it had but just started into daylight from some rocky cavity in the summit of Plinlimmon or Pen-

maen Mawr. The average temperature is about 56 degrees of Fahrenheit.

The SHOWER as well as the SHAMPOOING BATHS are
all as perfect and complete in their respective arrangements
as those of more simple construction; and the persons in
attendance are fully instructed in the proper methods of
their application. The same remarks will equally apply to
the VAPOUR and DOUCH BATHS for the local application
of steam, and of which there are several in this establishment. The shampooing and vapour baths are particularly
recommended by the faculty for the cure of paralysis, gouty
affections, rheumatism, lumbago, and other complaints affecting the limbs; as also for the removal of all cutaneous
disorders, or such as result from a languid circulation of
the blood, or from nervous debility.

THE HOT AIR AND STEAM BATHS.—These, which
are but modern inventions, have, notwithstanding, been
found to be highly beneficial in a great variety of disorders.
From an improper use of them being, however, attended
with considerable risk to the health of the patient, they
should never be had recourse to except by special medical
advice; indeed, the attendants at these baths are instructed
not to administer them, but in compliance with a physician's order. They may be employed either with simple
hot air or vapour, or else with volatilized impregnations
of chlorine, sulphur, and other mineral and vegetable substances. The apparatus of these baths is delicate and
complicated, and to the curious in such matters are not
altogether unworthy their examination. There has also
been lately introduced here one of La Beaume's AIR PUMP
VAPOUR BATHS, constructed upon the most improved
principle, and under the direction of the inventor. In their
cards, the proprietors of this establishment state that the

" hot air baths are on the same principle as those of the French institute at Paris, those at Dublin, and at Mr. Green's, London; with a flexible tube for the local application of chlorine and other gases."

The terms for bathing at the Montpellier Baths are as follow:

		s.	d.
Cold Plunging Bath	....	1	0
Warm or Cold Shower Bath	....	1	6
Warm Fresh Water Bath	....	2	0
Douch Bath	....	2	6
Warm Salt Water Bath	....	3	0
Sulphur Bath	....	3	0
Douch Vapour Bath	....	3	6
Medicated, Vapour, and Shampooing Bath	....	4	0
Hot Air, Sulphur, and Chlorine Baths	....	4	6

Where a number of baths are taken and assured by pre-payment, a slight reduction is made in the foregoing charges.

A third bathing establishment formerly existed in Regent Street, but, not succeeding, the premises have been long since converted to other purposes.

A mere enumeration of those disorders in which bathing has generally proved beneficial, would occupy a greater space in our little work than we could well afford to the subject; added to which, the practice has now become so universal, and its principles so thoroughly understood, that it would not only be out of place, but quite superfluous, to weary the reader with the details and minutiæ of diseases with which, we hope, he is neither afflicted himself, nor, perhaps, takes any interest in having discussed as a speculative question. If labouring under any really serious complaint, he would naturally hesitate at following the directions of non-medical guides, as to the policy of having recourse to, or abstaining from, the use of artificial baths;

and if he consider it merely as a question of luxury, it is more than probable that his own feelings alone will be consulted. We, therefore, dismiss the subject at once, satisfied with having directed him to where he may most readily obtain the different kinds of baths, for which either necessity or inclination may lead him to enquire.

Adjoining the Montpellier Baths is the LABORATORY for

THE REAL CHELTENHAM SALTS,

which, as being the only manufactory in the place, demands especial notice.

It has already been stated that, during the life-time of the late H. Thompson, Esq., above eighty wells had been sunk upon the Montpellier estate, all of which yielded an abundant supply of Mineral Waters; so abundant indeed that, judging from the success which had hitherto attended his discoveries, there was every reason to believe that Nature never intended to set bounds to her liberality. The supplies, which but a few years before had been found insufficient to furnish one hour's consumption to the drinkers, had suddenly become so exhaustless as to surpass the expectations of the most sanguine. Mr. Thompson, on finding himself in possession of such extensive resources, determined upon converting them to a more profitable account than he had hitherto done, and by changing the Spa Waters into Salts, remunerate himself for the great labour and expense which he had incurred in the undertaking, and at the same time afford an opportunity to persons who were prevented by circumstances from drinking the Waters at the wells, to avail themselves of the best possible substitute. For this purpose the above laboratory was erected, and furnished with every necessary chemical apparatus for converting

the Spa Waters into the more solid and portable form
of aperient salts. The wells which had been sunk in the
immediate neighbourhood of the pump room, and in the
fields beyond, were connected with each other by means of
leaden pipes (of which several thousand feet were laid
down), and forcing pumps fixed at regular distances, for
the purpose of driving the collected Waters through one
main pipe down to the Laboratory. The cost of these
preliminary preparations was necessarily very great, but
the result fully justified the outlay.

Arrived at the manufactory, the Waters are suffered
to flow into large reservoirs beneath the floors, whence
they are pumped up into the boilers for evaporation. This
process being continued for about seven days and nights,
the liquor is then drawn off into a large cistern placed in
the room beneath, where it remains until the lime, magnesia, and other earthy matter has been precipitated, after
which it is again pumped up into a second boiler, where,
at a heat below boiling, a further concentration takes
place, until the appearance of a pellicle upon the surface
of the saline fluid gives intimation of its being in a state
fit for crystallization. It is then drawn off and conveyed
to the crystallizing vessels, which are deep iron pans, five
feet in diameter, and lined at the bottom and in their
whole circumference with well seasoned elm or beech wood,
to prevent the salts from acquiring any stain. When these
vessels are filled, a number of loose sticks are laid to float
upon the surface of the liquor, for the salts to attach
themselves to, that the crystallization may be distinct, and
not in a confused mass, as it would otherwise be at the
bottom of the coolers.* When the crystallization, which

* See Brande and Parke's Treatise.

requires from two to five days, according to the season of the year and the state of the weather, is thought complete, the mother liquor is drawn off, and the salts show themselves in numerous beautiful clusters, covering the sticks and the whole interior of the vessels. The salts thus produced are now placed in square baskets to drain, preparatory to bottling, and are sold under the name of "Crystals of real Cheltenham Salts."

A further process is pursued with respect to these crystals, in order to prepare them for hot climates; for though they keep very well in their original form in our own and other cold countries, yet, when exposed to the action of tropical suns, they readily dissolve. To guard against this inconvenience, therefore, the crystals are, by drying, reduced into a state of efflorescence, or powder. The room in which this process is effected is heated by steam pipes, which travel along the shelves upon which the salts are deposited. The water of crystallization being driven off by the heat thus communicated, the rough salts soon become converted into a fine powder, which may now be exposed, with perfect impunity, to any changes of temperature, without the least chance of injury, or losing any of their valuable sanative properties. Persons who have been taking a course of the Spa Waters at Cheltenham, would do well upon leaving, to take some of these salts away with them; as, by occasionally using them at their own homes, they will contribute materially to confirm whatever re-establishment of health may have been effected by the use of the natural Mineral Waters, which ought never to be abruptly and entirely discontinued.

Besides the Crystals and Efflorescence above described, several other preparations of Cheltenham Salts are also procured from the evaporation of the Spa Waters.

CHAPTER VI.

————

PUBLIC AMUSEMENTS.

Evening Musical Promenades—Montpellier Gardens—Park Gardens—
Old Wells and Pittville Entertainments—Summer and Winter Balls—
Assembly Rooms—Master of the Ceremonies—Concerts—Theatrical
Amusements—Races—Hunting Appointments—the Club and Billiard
Rooms, &c.

WE have hitherto confined our observations to those subjects alone which have exercised a more direct influence upon the prosperity of Cheltenham, and have considered the reputation of the plan solely in reference to the claims which it has upon the invalid and the valetudinarian, who resort hither for the recovery of that health which, peradventure, they have been seeking diligently, though unsuccessfully, elsewhere. And this we did from a conviction that these subjects will ever be considered as the most important, and as such ought to occupy the most prominent place in a work purporting to be a " Stranger's Guide." Having, however, thus far, endeavoured to direct the attention of our invalid visitor to such matters as appeared to claim his especial notice, and to lay before him such information as seemed best calculated to further the main object of all his enquiries, we now proceed to give a succinct

account of those public amusements which have contributed so essentially to exalt our town in the opinion and
esteem of the man of fashion and the votary of pleasure.
The body having been restored to the possession of health,
and fitted for the enjoyment of its wonted recreations,
it is meet and proper that these should be again introduced
to its notice, that the mind, being thereby influenced by
its natural excitements, may be preserved from those
feelings of lassitude and listlessness which are almost
inseparable from a country life, or, indeed, upon a sudden
introduction into strange scenes, however gay.

Had we been writing this chapter thirty years ago, or
for a winter rather than a summer population, we should
have deemed it our incumbent duty to have placed the
Assembly Rooms in the van and front of our narrative;
but as neither of these is the case, we shall commence our
account of the public entertainments of Cheltenham with the

MUSICAL PROMENADES,

since they form a very principal feature in the established
summer pastimes of the place. We have already (p. 79)
offered a passing remark upon those of the morning, which,
though not unfrequently scenes of great gaiety, must be
viewed as the consequence of so large an assemblage of
water drinkers meeting together, rather than a distinct
and designed source of amusement; we shall therefore
not cumber our pages with any further notice of them
here.

THE EVENING PROMENADES are held either on the
grand walk of the Montpellier Pump Room, or in the
garden opposite, as circumstances and the seasons suggest
to the proprietor motives of preference. They commence
early in May, and are continued three or four times a

week, or even oftener when the weather permits, until the latter end of October. The band, consisting of seventeen performers, of whom we cannot speak in terms of too high praise, usually begin playing at seven or half-past seven o'clock, and conclude at about half-past nine. The selection of music embraces all the most celebrated and scientific compositions, as well of ancient as of modern times, appropriately arranged, and which are performed with great taste and ability. These selections are generally programmed before the promenade commences, so that the leader is unable to answer the calls of subscribers for particular pieces so readily in the evening as in the morning performances, when no particular scheme has to be followed, and he is left more at liberty to select as choice or the wishes of the company appear to dictate. If the weather prove fair, the attendance, generally, is very numerous, especially on Saturday evenings, which appear to be considered as peculiarly fashionable nights; and as the shadows of twilight gather round the scene, the Rotunda and promenade room, as well as the grand walk, are brilliantly lighted up, producing a beautiful and diorama-like effect upon the appearance of every surrounding object. So grateful, indeed, is this change of light, that it becomes hard to determine whether the artificial splendour, thus suddenly called into existence, be not more in harmony with the fairy scene than the garish reflections of a western sun. The crowd of fair and sylph-like forms seen gliding to and fro,—pleasure beaming in every eye, and the bloom of absolute, or the quivering flush of partial and returning health, brightening upon every countenance, recal to the imaginative mind those visions of primeval time, which have been hitherto supposed to have had existence only in the day-dreams of the poet, and the fables of the ancient mythologist. This animating scene has been described by a modern troubadour as follows:

" 'Tis evening, beautifully bland
   Her mists are gathering round;
I surely gaze on fairy land,
   And tread on fairy ground.

For, lo! a bright and splendid train
   Of forms surpassing fair;
And Music's captivating strain
   Comes borne upon the air.

Youth, beauty, here first learn to sip
   Enjoyment from the throng,
' The merry eye, the cherry lip,
   The passing pleasing tongue.' "

Cheltenham Lyrics and other Poems.

When the evenings are cold or damp, the band remove into the Rotunda after the first two or three tunes; and the company, upon such occasions, either promenade in the long room, or seat themselves round the interior. Should it rain at the time fixed for commencing, the performance is usually deferred.

In connexion with these twilight recreations we must here introduce to our "Stranger's" notice,

THE MONTPELLIER GARDENS.

Having had occasion two or three times already to make mention of them, it now behoves us to speak a little more at large in reference to their own individual attractions. These Gardens, which are situate immediately opposite the Pump Room, were laid out by P. Thompson, Esq., and subsequently improved by Messrs. R. W. & C. Jearrad. The former gentleman built, at the north-western end of the grounds, an extensive range of hot and green

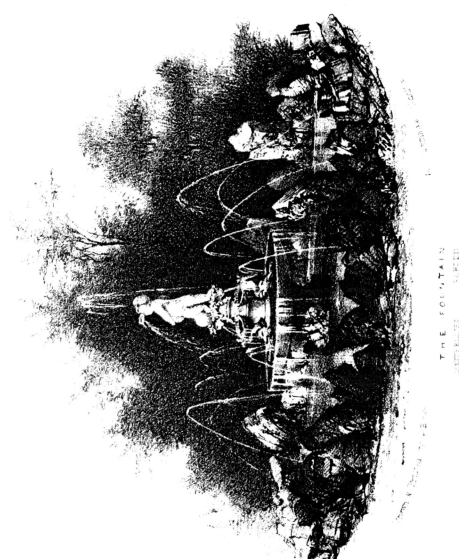

THE FOUNTAIN

houses, which are stocked with a large assortment of choice exotics and rare plants of every description. And to the latter gentlemen, who were lessees of the Montpellier establishment from 1831 to 1840, we are indebted for the light and elegant Chinese pagoda erected at the upper end of the Gardens, as also for the greater part of the plantations. In the pagoda the band was formerly stationed, but in 1841 Mr. P. Thompson, having purchased the galleries built for the famous Eglintoun tournament, erected a portion of them in the Montpellier Gardens as an orchestra; and here it is that the musical performances now constantly take place. On the lawn, in front of the conservatories, is a beautiful little MARBLE FOUNTAIN, removed from the Imperial Spa on the closing of that establishment, and which contributes greatly by the feeling of freshness that its presence induces, to the general effect of the scene. The design is that of a child grasping the throat of a swan, from whose mouth the water issues, as also from a circle of cherub-heads below. This little gem is the work of an Italian chisel; but, unfortunately, accident having deprived the swan of its original head, the loss has been supplied with more ingenuity than taste, by the carved the carved beak of an eagle.* During the long and warm evenings in June and July, the Musical Promenades are not unfrequently removed into these Gardens from the Grand Walk opposite. Similar arrangements are likewise adopted in the afternoons of autumn, when, the weather becoming cool and chilly, the EVENING entertainments are obliged to be discontinued, and the Band instead, performs from three to five o'clock in the afternoons.

* A legend, purporting to give the history of the Marble Fountain, was published in the *Cheltenham Looker-On* some years back, and has been since transferred to the " Cheltenham Album."

Upon public anniversaries, exhibitions of fireworks and other gala performances take place here; but as these depend entirely upon circumstances, no particular description can be given of them.

The Gardens are open every day (Sundays excepted) throughout the season, from ten in the morning to five in the afternoon for those subscribers to the Musical Promenades, who also pay the additional charge for liberty to exercise this privilege during the hours above named. The following are the

TERMS OF SUBSCRIPTION:

	To the Musical Promenades only.			To the Musical Promenades, with the use of the Gardens, Walks, & Rides.		
	£	s	d	£	s	d
Family for the Season	1	11	6	2	2	0
Two Months......	1	1	0	1	12	6
One Month	0	15	0	1	1	0
Two Persons for the Season....	1	1	0	1	10	0
Two Months ..	0	15	0	1	5	0
One Month ..	0	10	0	0	17	6
One Person for the Season	0	15	0	1	0	0
Two Months	0	10	0	0	12	6
One Month	0	5	0	0	7	0

Single Admission, 1s. each, to the Gardens or the Promenades.

The Musical Promenades may be subscribed for separately from the Gardens, but none save those who subscribe to the former can become subscribers to the latter.

No servant of any description is allowed to come upon the walk during the hours of the promenade, nor into the Gardens at any time.

Dogs are likewise prohibited.

THE PARK GARDENS

are situate about a quarter of a mile south of the Montpellier Spa, occupying the centre of the Park estate. They are laid out with very great taste, and with a stricter attention to the principles of landscape gardening than is usually found in public works of the kind; possessing also many natural advantages such as are not enjoyed by any other establishment in Cheltenham. Originally they were intended for Zoological Gardens, having been planned in 1837-8 by a joint-stock company started for that purpose; but the expenses of the undertaking having very considerably exceeded the income, the design was shortly abandoned, and the property sold to S. W. Daukes, Esq., who has converted the Gardens into public pleasure grounds. Of the entire area of twenty acres, comprised in this purchase, about fourteen are laid out in promenades and lawns, among flower beds and clumps of the choicest shrubs, having a beautiful sheet of water near the centre, and a romantic little rockery at the lower end. The remaining portion of the land on the south-east of the principal walk is set apart for cricket, archery, and other athletic sports. The Gardens are completely enclosed by a belt of fine plantation, which most effectually excludes the view from all persons outside. The entrance is on the north side, between Tivoli and Hatherley Place, which thoroughfares lead into the Park Drive. The Gardens are open daily (Sundays excepted) from nine o'clock till dusk; and strangers are charged one shilling for admission, except upon occasion of any extraordinary amusement, when an entrance-fee, varying with the kind and quality of the entertainment to be given, is demanded.

Besides the Montpellier and Park Gardens here noticed,

H

the lawns and pleasure grounds of the Royal Old Wells and the Pittville Spa are, in fine weather, much frequented for recreation and delightful exercise; and scenes of gaiety are often to be witnessed at both, which quite equal those of the two establishments just described: Fêtes and Galas are, indeed, of frequent occurrence at the Old Wells; and at Pittville the Floral Exhibitions, an occasional Public Breakfast, and now and then entertainments of a more musical character, attract numbers of our fashionable visitors to its fairy land, notwithstanding its distance from the town.

THE SUMMER BALLS

usually take place in the Montpellier Rotunda, every Thursday evening, from July to October. They were first established in 1826, and for many years were among the most attractive and elegant of the amusements of the season, but their brilliancy has been, for some time past, upon the wane. The change which the fashion of attending public assemblies has, of late years, undergone, and in part also, the alterations which have taken place in the arrangements of the rooms themselves, rendering these less commodious than they originally were, have, no doubt, contributed largely to this result. Still, during the height of the season, the Summer Promenade Balls afford an agreeable variety to the established amusements of the place, and are attended by many of the leading families, as well residents as visitors. Their style and character differ in many particulars from the Balls of other establishments, with the regulations of which the public has been long familiarized. They commence, for instance, at half-past eight, and terminate at the early hour of half-past eleven. The formality of full dress is dispensed with; ladies indeed

are especially invited to attend in promenade costume, the
rule as to gentlemen being that they shall be in "full
evening dress." The Rotunda is appropriated to dancing,
an orchestra being erected over the pump case for the
reception of the band, and the general interior of the
building being decorated suitably and in character with
the intended amusement. Refreshments, consisting of
tea and coffee, are served to the company in the long
room, free of any charge, extra that of the admission,
which varies from three to five shillings each for non-subscribers. To parties who subscribe for the series, the rate
of admission-charge is very considerably less.

THE WINTER BALLS

are held at the Assembly Rooms, the series generally
commencing in the month of December, and terminating
about the end of March or beginning of April;—frequently
with the Ball which takes place on Easter Monday. The
same regulations obtain for the most part at these as at the
Summer assemblies; though a fuller style of dress is generally adopted, and the dancing does not open or close at
quite such early hours. Besides the regular Balls here
spoken of, there are generally, about mid-winter, one or
two Fancy Balls got up by the bachelors and hunting
gentlemen, who take this method of returning the kindness
and courtesies of the residents, of whose hospitalities
they have been participators during the period of their
temporary sojourn in the place. These "extraordinaries"
are invariably very brilliant affairs.

Both the Summer and the Winter Balls are conducted
under the sanction and cognizance of an honorary committee, composed of a number of the most influential resident gentlemen of Cheltenham, to whom all matters of

doubt and disagreement connected with the regulations and conduct of these public assemblies are referred. But by far the most important officer, as regards the right conduct and tone of these elegant and long favourite amusements of the fashionable circles of society, is

THE MASTER OF THE CEREMONIES,

whose special office and duty it is to direct and preside over the public Balls; and to afford such information connected with the rules and regulations applying thereto, as strangers may require for their guidance. This appointment is at present filled by Capt. A. H. Kirwan, who was elected in 1835. It is the general practice of the Master of the Ceremonies to call upon the visitors as soon after their arrival as their residence can be ascertained, and it is considered etiquette to return the call. In order to enable him to pay them this mark of attention and respect, it is particularly desirable that, on entering their names in any of the subscription books of the Spas or Libraries, or in the general arrival book kept at the Montpellier Library, the addresses should be uniformly added, as without some such intimation it is now frequently impossible, the town having become so large, to find out the residences of strangers. The official duties of the Master of the Ceremonies are strictly limited to the Ball Room, beyond which he possesses no authority. It is his province to introduce partners for the different dances that are called; but where parties, wholly unknown to him, desire such introductions, they should avail themselves of the intermediation of a mutual friend, on making known their wishes to the M.C., from whom they will, at all times, receive the most prompt and courteous attention. Where no opportunity of such formal introduction has occurred, it is not

thought out of etiquette in subscribers introducing themselves either in the ball room, on the promenade, or in any
of the places of fashionable public resort. Subscription
Books are open for the Master of the Ceremonies at the
different Spas, the Assembly Rooms, and Libraries, and at
the principal Hotels of the town, in which it is customary
for visitors, desirous of paying him a compliment, to enter
their names—the usual subscription being one guinea.
The Master of the Ceremonies has an annual summer ball
at the Montpellier Rotunda, generally in September, and
a winter ball at the Assembly Rooms in January. Tickets
for admission to these balls are generally sent to the subscribers.

Having spoken of the Winter Balls, we now proceed
to notice

THE ASSEMBLY ROOMS

in which they are held: they are situated on the south side
of the High Street, between Cambray and the Plough
Hotel, and, from the extent of frontage which they present, and the projecting portico, form rather a striking
feature in this part of the town.

We find, as early as 1780, when Mr. Moreau was first
appointed Master of the Ceremonies of Cheltenham, or
very soon after, that there were two public rooms, in which
dancing and card parties alternated nightly throughout the
season: they were called the Upper and Lower Rooms.
These having revelled through their day, were succeeded,
in 1810, by more commodious premises built on the scite
of the present establishment, which was erected, in 1815-16,
by J. D. Kelly, Esq., at a cost of between fifty and sixty
thousand pounds. The Ball Room is considered to be one
of the best in England, measuring eighty-seven feet long

by forty feet wide, and forty high, and is lighted by eleven elegant glass chandeliers. The ceiling and cornice are elaborately decorated, and the sides of the room are broken into compartments by a series of well-proportioned pilasters. The orchestra for the band is placed in the centre of the west wall, and a neat gallery crosses one end immediately above the folding doors opening into the room in front, which, on ball nights, is appropriated to cards and the usual refreshments. Up stairs two large and handsome apartments, extending through the entire frontage of the building, are occupied by the Cheltenham and Gloucestershire Club; but these are generally available to the purposes of any extraordinary fête, being freely lent for such occasions by the members of the club. The Assembly Rooms were first opened on the 29th of July, 1816, when the Duke of Wellington and other distinguished and illustrious characters honoured them with their presence. Besides the Ball and Club Rooms, above described, there are also two excellent Billiard Rooms, and two or three others which are let for various exhibitions, or leased for warerooms. The establishment is, at present, the property of a joint stock company, who let out the premises to different parties,—the Ball, Club, and Billiard Rooms including as these necessarily do, all other public amusements, forming the principal tenancy.

Among the purposes to which the Assembly Rooms are most frequently applied, are

PUBLIC CONCERTS,

of which several generally take place in course of the year. At the close of the London season the most eminent artists of the Italian opera usually pay Cheltenham an early professional visit, and seldom leave it without reaping an ample reward for the gratification they afford. Besides these the resident professors frequently speculate in vocal or instrumental performances—the number of highly talented musicians connected with the public bands, who are permanently abiding in the town, affording great facilities for filling up the different departments of an orchestra. For entertainments of these descriptions the large Assembly Room is admirably adapted, being capable of accommodating from four to six hundred persons, according as the seats may be arranged. The Montpellier Rotunda is also occasionally let for public Concerts, and for Summer *Morning* performances the preference is generally given to it, from its more cool and airy appearance.

THEATRICAL AMUSEMENTS

were formerly of regular occurrence in Cheltenham, and a Theatre constituted, for nearly half a century, one of its most certain places of amusement and recreation. But the taste for the drama, like that for public Balls, has, of late years, much declined, and is not likely, very soon, to experience a revival. The famous John Kemble and his sister, Mrs. Siddons, in the early part of their career, not unfrequently acted in Cheltenham, in a temporary playhouse, which has since been converted into the York Hotel. The success which attended the representations of that day induced a Mr. J. Watson, in 1805, to erect a permanent building in Cambray. In this, which was an exceedingly neat and commodious little Theatre, nearly all the distinguished actors of the last forty years, at one time or other, appeared before the Cheltenham public; but its palmiest recollections were associated with a party of amateurs, of which the present Earl Fitzhardinge, then Col. Berkeley, and his brothers, the Hons. Frederick and Augustus

Berkeley, were the principal performers. These gentlemen, for many years, kept up the Cheltenham Theatre almost entirely by their exertions; and when, on the exaltation of Col. Berkeley to the peerage, the party became broken up, the fashion for dramatic entertainments underwent a complete change. The house, erewhile, too small for the audiences which thronged for admission within its walls, became suddenly " a world too wide" for all the ordinary demands upon its capacity; and an accident which totally destroyed the building by fire, in May, 1839, saved it from the more inglorious end to which it was obviously hastening. Since the destruction of the theatre several attempts have been made to re-establish dramatic entertainments in the town, particularly one made in the winter of 1841-2, at the Assembly Rooms, where a temporary stage, fitted up with suitable scenery and machinery, was erected. But each effort has proved more abortive than its precursor; and a theatre in Cheltenham will, probably, remain for yet many years—a desideratum.

Among other pastimes catered for the amusement of the summer visitor, not the least important are the

PUBLIC RACES,

which usually take place in the month of June or July. The first attempt at introducing these popular English sports into Cheltenham, was made in 1818—the ground selected for the experiment being Nottingham Hill. The result proving successful, it was determined to continue them annually, and a course was marked out on Cleeve Hill for the purpose, where, with one or two exceptions, they have ever since been held. The Grand Stand, erected some eight or ten years ago, on the very top of the hill, may be distinctly seen from almost any part of the town.

The shortest route to the course is through Prestbury, but the best and only passable road for carriages is up the London road as far as Andoversford, and then turning to the left through the village of Whittington, along the Cotteswolds. The distance to the course is, by the latter route, about nine miles, and by the former not more than six. There are generally two days' sports. The crack race of the first day is the *Gloucestershire Stakes,* and that of the second the *Cheltenham Gold Cup.*

Besides the regular races noted above, there has been, for some years past, what is termed a *Spring Meeting,* at which STEEPLE CHASES and private matches constitute the usual sporting attractions. This meeting is held about the end of March or beginning of April, towards the close of the hunting season, its principal supporters being the gentlemen of the Berkeley Hunt Club—a sporting fraternity —the members of which have periodical dinners at the Plough Hotel, whereat are discussed the arrangements of the chase and the turf connected with the neighbourhood of Cheltenham and the county.

THE HUNTING APPOINTMENTS

are a source of great attraction during the winter months, and induce many families to take up their residence in Cheltenham from October to April; having the promise of congenial occupation. The celebrated Fox Hounds of Earl Fitzhardinge come up from Berkeley Castle the 1st of November, and hunt the Cotteswold and Broadway countries all that month, as also January and March. The appointments of the pack are on the most princely scale, and there are few keener sportsmen than its noble owner, who is uniformly accompanied by an excellent and splendid field. The meets are generally published in the newspapers a week in advance. The principal covers drawn by Lord Fitzhardinge's hounds are the following:

Badgworth	Guiting Woods	Queen Wood
Chatcomb	Hawling Wood	Rencomb Park
Chedworth Wood	Hazleton Brake	Rencomb Side
Cliffordine	——— Gorse	Short Wood
Coomb End	Hilcot	Sidebottom
Corndean Plantations	Humble-bee-how	Stancomb
Cowley	Leckhampton Gorse	Star Wood
Dixon Wood	Lineover	Stoke Brake
Dowdeswell	Litcomb	Westwood
Down Hatherley	Monkham	Withington Wood
Dumbleton	Moorwood	Winchcomb Side
Greet Grove	Puckham Scrubbs	Winnyates Brake

There has been for the last few years a subscription pack of Stag Hounds, which in the months of October, December, and February, has gone out generally two or three times a-week, and in the alternate months occasionally on the Fridays; on which day Earl Fitzhardinge's hounds never hunt, being *en route* to Broadway, which is his Lordship's meet every Saturday.

The Duke of Beaufort's and Lord Ducie's hounds frequently approach within ten or twelve miles of Cheltenham; and in the months when Earl Fitzhardinge's pack is absent, the meets of these noblemen are attended by many of the Nimrods of the Cotteswolds.

A private pack of Harriers, kept by W. E. Lawrence, Esq., of the Greenway, hunt the winter through, and contribute to the amusement of many of the gentry of the neighbourhood, who require not the more stimulating excitement of Fox or Stag Hounds to afford them pleasure.

THE CHELTENHAM & GLO'STERSHIRE CLUB

has been established many years, and is supported by the

leading nobility and gentry of the town and neighbourhood. Members of the principal London clubs are eligible
to admission without the form of election, but all others
have to be ballotted for; and visitors, unless already connected with some similar metropolitan establishment, require the introduction of two members. The terms of
subscription are:

	£	s.	d.
For One Year	3	3	0
For a Month	1	6	0

The suite of apartments appropriated to the use of the
Club extends along the whole first floor of the Assembly
Rooms. Attached to the Club is an excellent Billiard
Room, appropriated to the exclusive use of the members.
There are also several other

BILLIARD ROOMS

in the town, not restricted as to their admissions. That
on the ground-floor of the Assembly Rooms is the oldest
and most frequented; it is furnished with Hunt's patent
metallic table, and is said to be convenient in its arrangements, and well conducted. The NEW BILLIARD ROOMS,
situated in the opening between the Colonnade and Regent
Street, was next established, and enjoys a fair share of patronage. The establishment consists of a subscribers' and
a non-subscribers' room, which are lighted by skylights.
There are patent tables in both. In 1841-2 Billiard Rooms
were opened contiguous to the Montpellier Rotunda, fitted
up in a very superior style, and possessing every advantage calculated to render them attractive. There are also
other Billiard Rooms in the town; but the above constitute the only ones much resorted to by gentlemen
players.

Besides the objects of attraction above enumerated,

and which must be considered as the permanent and established amusements of the town, there are always a great
number of fluctuating entertainments, which tarry here so
long as they meet with encouragement and support, with-
drawing themselves to other places when these fail, and
leaving the field again vacant for other adventurers. Of
the sights and exhibitions which in this way visit Cheltenham, during the season, it is of course impossible for us
to give any account; and as the visitor will always have
due notice given him of these things, by the newspapers
and through the other customary mediums of public announcement, it is perhaps as unnecessary as it is impossible.

CHAPTER VII.

FINE ARTS, SCIENCE, AND LITERATURE.

*Lord Northwick's Picture Gallery—Literary and Philosophical Institution—Floral and Horticultural Association—*NEWSPAPERS—*the Cheltenham Chronicle, Journal, Looker-On, Free Press, Examiner, Bath and Cheltenham Gazette—*SUBSCRIPTION LIBRARIES—*the Montpellier, Williams's, Lee's, Lovesy's.*

LEST our visitor should imagine that Cheltenham, while sedulously improving all its local advantages, and multiplying its amusements, has been solicitous only for the advancement of individual prosperity or the gratification of the senses, we shall now proceed to introduce to his notice, those establishments, the professed object of which is to cater for the intellectual pleasures of society, as well as to furnish entertainment for those whose dispositions lead them not to mingle in the glitter and gaiety of fashionable life, aspiring to more cultivated and refined enjoyments. Such persons will find in the public Institutions of the town much to afford them gratification, and in our Subscription Libraries the amplest sources of general information. The latter are all of them conducted with great spirit and liberality, and possess most of those attractions so essential to the student and the man of letters, whose

habits and inclinations peradventure unfit them for the
enjoyment of amusements congenial to the feelings of a
worshipper at the shrine of fashion.

Before, however, we proceed to speak of either public
Institutions or Libraries, or of other matters connected with
the state of science or literature, we must introduce our
strangers to

THIRLESTANE HOUSE,

THE PICTURE GALLERY OF LORD NORTHWICK,

which, to persons of refined taste, and who are also possessed of a love for the fine arts, will, assuredly, prove an
object of peculiar interest and early attraction—few private
collections in the kingdom equalling this, either in the
number, richness, or variety of their contents, and none
being so accessible to the public. Through the generous
courtesy of its noble proprietor, the gallery of Thirlestane
House is generally open from one to four o'clock daily,
Sundays, of course, excepted; the only form of introduction required being the entry of the visitor's name in a
book kept for that purpose. This privilege is, however,
partially suspended when Lord Northwick is in Cheltenham. At such times permission to view the Paintings in
the Gallery, and private apartments connected therewith,
can only be obtained by an application to his Lordship;
but an application, respectfully made, is rarely refused,
even where the parties are strangers. The Gallery is also
closed to all visitors in very wet or dirty weather, a re-
striction no less necessary to be observed for the sake of
the Paintings themselves than for the polished or carpetted
floors of the different apartments, inasmuch as it is impossible that the former can be seen to fair advantage in
unfavourable lights.

The noble mansion here spoken of is situated in the Bath road, and was purchased by its present owner from the executors of the late Mr. Scott, who is reported to have spent about eighty thousand pounds in its erection, but who died while yet the building was in an incomplete state, particularly the interior. Lord Northwick has, however, not merely completed what Mr. Scott left unfinished, but has also made important additions to the original design. The five large rooms which occupy the ground-floor fronts of the principal building, have been elegantly furnished, and the walls of the entire suite hung with paintings by the most eminent masters, presenting an array of artist talent of surpassing rarity. Besides all this his lordship has thrown out from the eastern side of his mansion a separate structure, for the express purposes of a Picture Gallery, connecting this wing to the main building by a small circular apartment, in which many choice gems of taste and virtu are placed, as well as some of the smaller cabinet pictures. The gallery is lighted by a series of skylights. Its length is 80 feet, its breadth 26, and its height 29 feet; but as the three principal rooms open into immediate display with the gallery, the entire length viewed through from the extremity of the latter is 210 feet. Of the rich and rare contents of this splendid suite of apartments it is impossible to speak in terms of adequate praise, the walls being enriched with the productions of some of the most eminent masters of the chief schools of painting, as well native as foreign. Among the former are examples of the works of Etty, Mulready, Roberts, Creswick, Hart, and others of equal celebrity; and among the former are several splendid specimens of Rubens, Velasquez, Guido, Berghem, Salvator Rosa, Carlo Dolce, and other choice names in the catalogue of continental *illustrissimi*.

THE LITERARY AND PHILOSOPHICAL INSTITUTION.

THE LITERARY AND PHILOSOPHICAL INSTITUTION,

in the line of the Promenade Villas, is a structure of bold and classical appearance, having a handsome portico, modelled after that of the Temple of Theseus, and supported by six fluted columns. The building was erected in 1835-6, from designs by R. W. Jearrad, Esq., the talented architect of Christ Church, the Queen's Hotel, and others of the most modern buildings of Cheltenham. The interior consists of a Lecture Room, measuring 55 feet by 28, and lighted by three large skylights; contiguous are a Laboratory and a Committee Room, and over these a small Museum, in which are collected many curious and interesting objects of natural history. The Library department of the establishment, though in its infancy, contains many valuable works—already amounting to several hundred volumes; and the principal Reviews and Periodicals are taken in for the use of the members, who are entitled to the entry of the Reading Room, which is open daily from ten o'clock till nine in the evening.

The society to whom the building and property belong, was established in 1833. It consists of proprietors, annual subscribers, and life and honorary members. The shares are of £50, £35, and £20, each; the rights and privileges attaching to each of which are, of course, corresponding to the amounts respectively represented. The annual subscribers are of one or two guineas each, according to the advantages sought to be obtained.

The professed objects of the society are the formation of a permanent Library of Reference, the delivery of Literary and Scientific Lectures, and the promotion of intellectual pursuits generally. The session for public lec-

I

tures extends from September to May. The lectures are mostly delivered in the evenings, though there appears to be no fixed rule for this arrangement.

The management of the Institution is undertaken by a president, vice-president, treasurer, honorary secretary, and a council of fifteen members, who are all elected at the annual meeting held in March. The property is vested in twelve trustees—the whole being duly enrolled in Chancery.

———

The Church of England Working Men's Association is a literary and scientific institution, designed, as its name implies, for the humbler classes—members of the Church of England. The society was established in 1839; is under the presidentship of the Rev. F. Close, who with the other officers, and a committee of twelve members, are the managers of its affairs and directors of its proceedings. The annual subscription is 4s., which entitles to the lectures and the use of a reading room, open in the evenings after half-past six o'clock. The rooms of the Association are in St. George's Place.

Besides the above, a Mechanics' Institution has still nominal existence in Albion Street; but its professed objects have been, of late, so perverted to political purposes, that it now scarcely deserves to be catalogued at all among places of scientific or literary instruction.

———

THE CHELTENHAM FLORAL AND HORTICULTURAL ASSOCIATION,

a society having for its objects the promoting a taste for the most elegant and captivating of the departments of botanical study. It has been established now for some years, and, being well supported and encouraged, has exercised a beneficial influence upon the state of floriculture in and around Cheltenham. Under the auspices of the association five or six exhibitions are held during the summer, alternately at the Montpellier and Pittville Spas, which are usually very gay affairs, being patronized by the leading gentry of the town and neighbourhood. At these exhibitions premiums and prizes are awarded for the finest specimens of the different plants, fruits, and flowers, in season. A subscription of 10s. 6d. per annum constitutes a member of the society, and admits to the exhibitions, with liberty to introduce a friend. The affairs of the association are managed by a committee, treasurer, and secretary; from any of whom any further particulars required may be learnt.

———

Next to those Institutions already described, which have for their immediate objects the cultivation of literature and science, and the spread of knowledge in some one or other of its numerous departments, we may here notice the

PUBLIC NEWSPAPERS

which are published in the town. Of these there are, at the present time, not less than five.

THE CHELTENHAM CHRONICLE & GLO'STERSHIRE ADVERTISER, was the first established, being commenced in 1809, when as yet the population numbered only about 7000. It is published on Thursday, or rather on Wednesday evening, being printed off sufficiently early to admit of transmission by the over-night's post. It was formerly considered a whig paper; but of late years its opinions have undergone a change, and it is now the advocate of conservative principles. In its columns especial attention is paid to theological controversies, and to questions of church government; and they generally also contain very full reports of religious meetings. The department of local intelligence is usually well filled with notices of passing events; and there is a fair space devoted to matters of general interest. *The Chronicle* has ever had the largest circulation of all the Cheltenham papers. The Office of publication is in Pittville Street.

THE CHELTENHAM JOURNAL, the second weekly " broadsheet" issued for the enlightenment of the inhabitants, was begun in 1824; and professes, like the *Chronicle,* conservative opinions. It affords the customary information on all occurrences of local interest; and gives a digest of the metropolitan news of the week. Its circulation is limited. It is published on Monday mornings, at the Office in Queen's Buildings, near the Royal Hotel.

THE CHELTENHAM LOOKER-ON, " a Note Book of Fashionable Sayings and Doings," is an octavo sheet, published every Saturday morning, (price three pence, stamped), at the Montpellier Library. It enjoys an extensive circulation among the visitors and resident gentry of the place, to whose movements and amusements it is most particularly devoted; noticing the Balls and other public entertainments which take place more fully and accurately than any of its contemporaries. The arrivals, changes, and departures, which are continually occurring in a place like Cheltenham, are carefully registered in its pages. Its " leader " is devoted to the " gossip " of the Court, which is always faithfully and entertainingly reported by a London correspondent. The *Looker-On* also frequently contains literary and scientific papers of considerable ability, and original sketches of society, contributed generally by writers of established reputation. An AR-RIVAL BOOK is open at the Montpellier Library for receiving the names of visitors, whence they are transferred to the pages of the *Looker-On*. This paper was established in 1833.

THE CHELTENHAM FREE PRESS, published every Saturday morning, was started in 1834, and is the champion of ultra-liberal opinions. The tone of its political articles is bold and uncompromising; and much ability is sometimes displayed in the advocacy of the particular views which it maintains. It enjoys a respectable circulation among the advocates and supporters of the ballot, universal suffrage, and "the charter." The Office of the *Free Press* is at No. 318, High Street.

THE CHELTENHAM EXAMINER, the last established of our newspapers, was commenced in 1839, as the organ of the whig party in the town, by whom the extremes of the *Free Press* were repudiated. It is quite a political paper, discussing the measures of goverment with partizan zeal. It is conducted with considerable talent, has a circulation next to the *Cheltenham Chronicle* in amount, and is the largest sheet, measured by the scale of "superficial inches," of all the Cheltenham newspapers. The Office of the *Examiner* is in Clarence Street: it is published early on Wednesday mornings.

Besides the newspapers just enumerated there are also three others, having a sort of half connection with the place; these are

THE BATH AND CHELTENHAM GAZETTE, which is devoted principally to the affairs of that ancient city, but it contains also brief notices of the events occurring in the latter borough, though generally consisting of compilations from the Cheltenham papers. To persons equally interested in, or curious about the doings of both places, the *Bath and Cheltenham Gazette* will prove an useful and acceptable journal. It is published in Bath on Tuesday, and reaches Cheltenham on Wednesday morning.

THE GLOUCESTER JOURNAL and the GLOUCESTER-SHIRE CHRONICLE—the one a whig, the other a tory, in politics—are both admirably conducted papers, and have extensive circulations. Each has an agent in Cheltenham, and reports such proceedings connected with its welfare as are likely to prove generally interesting. They are published early on Saturday morning.

Having thus noticed the newspapers which undertake to furnish intelligence of what passes in our own immediate neighbourhood, as well as throughout the kingdom at large, we now proceed to enumerate those establishments in which strangers will be always sure to find them awaiting perusal, together with those of most other parts of the country; and at the same time enjoy the use of extensive Circulating Libraries, whence to select " reading for the hours of retirement."

THE MONTPELLIER LIBRARY

is situated at the upper end of the grand promenade, and adjoining the Rotunda. There is also an entrance at the back of the pump room, off the high road leading to Lansdowne Place. From its advantageous situation this establishment is much resorted to during the summer season, as well by the man of fashion as by the invalid, who here escapes the noise and stir inseparable from the town. All the London daily and most of the weekly newspapers are taken in for the use of the subscribers to the reading room, which is also provided with several of the provincial ones, together with the leading reviews, magazines, and other literary journals. The library comprehends a well selected collection of the most modern publications in history, biography, romance, and general literature. The *Cheltenham Looker-On* is published here every Saturday morning.

WILLIAMS'S ENGLISH AND FOREIGN LIBRARY

adjoins and forms part of the eastern end of the Assembly Rooms. The catalogue of this establishment shows a most extensive collection of works in every branch of English literature, history, biography, voyages and travels, novels, romances, &c. &c. It also comprehends a variety of the most popular productions of the continental press. The reading rooms, which are placed in the rear of the shop, are regularly supplied with the principal London and provincial newspapers, reviews, magazines, and other literary and political journals; and all the newest and most popular publications of the day are added to the circulating library as soon as published. Mr. Williams's collection of old and rare books for sale, is well worthy the attention of the bibliomaniac and the lover of " scarce editions."

LEE'S ROYAL LIBRARY,

No. 384, High Street, and nearly opposite the George Hotel, was the first public circulating library established in Cheltenham. Its situation is particularly eligible and convenient, and the reading room, which is eighty feet in length, and looks out into a pleasant shrubbery at the back, forms one of the most airy and pleasant summer retreats in the town. It is abundantly supplied with newspapers, magazines, and reviews, as well provincial as metropolitan; and the circulating library contains a valuable selection of standard works, as well as all new and interesting publications of the day, in every department of literature. This establishment has always obtained a very liberal share of public patronage, and every thing is done by its present proprietor to ensure a continuance thereof.

LOVESY'S LIBRARY,

Promenade Villas, nearly opposite the Imperial Hotel, is fitted up with every attention to the comfort and convenience of its subscribers. It is well supplied with the new publications, and the reading room, which is over the library, with most of the London and several of the provincial journals.

The London morning newspapers are received at all the above Reading Rooms early in the afternoon of the day of publication, and the evening papers at eight o'clock the following morning. The terms of subscription to these establishments range from two to five guineas per annum, being graduated according to the number of persons frequenting the reading rooms, and the works required at home. When parties subscribe for shorter periods than the year, the scale of charge is proportionably higher. Books are only lent to subscribers.

CHAPTER VIII.

CHURCHES AND CHAPELS.

St. Mary's—New Burial Ground—Trinity—St. John's—St. James's—St. Paul's—Christ Church—St. Philip's—Cheltenham Chapel—Wesleyan Methodist Chapels—Baptist Chapels—Portland—Highbury—Quakers'—Roman Catholic—Unitarian Chapels—Jews' Synagogue, &c.

FEW towns of equal extent in the kingdom possess so many churches and chapels as Cheltenham, or can boast so efficient and devoted a body of clergy, both in and out of the establishment. Zealous and indefatigable in the discharge of the important duties which, as messengers of the Gospel, they are called upon to perform, and ever labouring to extend the sphere of its holy influence, their ceaseless aim is to implant deeply and permanently in the hearts and affections of their flocks the sacred principles of eternal truth. Nor do they leave any Christian effort untried which seems calculated to further the advancement of that religion whereof they are the appointed ministers; and which, in their hands, vested with the power of Ithuriel's spear, strips off its panoply from vice and falsehood, and exposes at a touch the foul deformity of specious virtue. But, as they aim at higher objects than that of obtaining the praises of men, we shall abstain

from any further observations upon the subject, and proceed the rather to a brief account of those sacred edifices,
over which they are severally called upon to preside.

ST. MARY'S CHURCH.

This, which is the parish church, and comprehended
in the deanery of Winchcomb, is a very ancient and
beautiful structure, and, as an object of curiosity alone,
deserves the particular attention of every visitor of Cheltenham, especially if he be an admirer of the noble works
achieved by his forefathers, in the olden time, and when

gothic architecture was in its "high and palmy state."
It is situated on the south-west of the High Street, some
hundred yards or so in the rear of the Magistrates' Office,
on each side of which is an avenue leading directly to the
northern entrance. From the best evidence which antiquaries have been able to collect on this subject, it appears
that its establishment must have taken place early in the
eleventh century, and tradition ascribes to the year 1011
the honour of its erection.

In 1133 Henry the First granted the impropriation to
the Abbey of Cirencester. At the dissolution of monasteries it reverted to the crown. From that period to 1624
it was leased by several persons, among the number of
whom was the illustrious Francis Bacon, who, in consideration of the sum of £75 18s. 4d. obtained a grant of the
curacy for forty years. In 1624 Sir Baptist Hicks became
seised of the living, and a decree in Chancery was obtained,
compelling the impropriator to allow £40 a-year to the
officiating minister. Sir Baptist vested the nomination in
Jesus College, Oxford. The impropriation has subsequently passed through a variety of hands, and is now the
property of six trustees, who, in 1816, purchased it for
the sum of three thousand pounds.

The church itself is a spacious cruciform structure,
with a spire in the centre, and is remarkable for the richness and variety displayed in the tracery of its windows,
particularly one of the round or " rose " form in the north
transept, fifteen feet in diameter, and containing thirty-
three glazed compartments. This window is shown in the
above view of St. Mary's church, engraved from a drawing by Prout. The north aisle has an interior porch, or
large door-way, the carved enrichments of which are very
elegant, of the reign of Edward the Third. Among them

is a knight, in bas-relief, encountering a wild beast; the
situation of this figure in a spandril, as well as the general
execution of the whole, forcibly recal to mind the celebrated monument of the same age in Beverley minster,
called, *par eminence*, the " Percy Shrine." The south porch,
which is of much more recent date, is decorated internally
with crocketed pinnacles and other enrichments. Its position was, originally, occupied by a large window, which has
been broken through for its introduction: over this porch
the upper portion of the window still remains. In the contiguous south wall is an elegant niche, which was evidently
the ancient baptistery; the hole by which the font was fixed
therein still remains.   In the chancel also, near the altar, is
a singular piece of ancient sculpture; it is a small square
canopy of stone, perhaps a reliquary, or shrine; the carv-
ings round it represent priests. Rick-
man calls this " a very handsome water
drain of decorated character, and not
common shape;" describing it as " a
square recess, with buttresses and an
arch on the east and north sides, with
a good crocketed canopy—having an
embattled top, the underside of which
is groined."* The altar-piece is an
elaborate specimen of " carved oak
furniture," presented to the church by
the Dean and Chapter of Gloucester; and though, doubtless, highly esteemed in the age in which it was manufactured, accords not with the taste of the present day in
ecclesiastical affairs. The frame-work is surmounted by
gilt cherubs, and a golden sun projected upon a sky-blue
ground; and other " decorations" equally inappropriate

* Rickman's Gothic Architecture, p. 171.

in style to the sacred character of the edifice. In the north
aisle is the arched recess of an ancient monument; but all
its former contents have been removed or concealed, in
order to increase the seats of the pew. The church, and
the adjacent churchyard, abound with sepulchral memorials
belonging to families of rank and respectability.

The exterior remains still in nearly its original state,
but the interior has from time to time undergone considerable alterations, rendered necessary as the increase of population demanded a more economical disposition of the
sittings. The late Rev. C. Jervis bestowed great attention
upon the internal improvements of the church, and by
introducing something like system into the arrangements,
contributed materially to the convenience and comfort of
the congregation. The organ, which was erected by public
subscription in 1810, is esteemed a finely toned instrument; and the bells, ten in number, as well tuned a peal as,
perhaps, with very few exceptions, is to be met with in any
town in the kingdom. The present incumbent of St.
Mary's is the Rev. F. Close, whose popularity as a preacher
is surpassed only by his exemplary and christian-like conduct in private life, and his active zeal and unwearied
efforts in support of the different benevolent institutions
in the town, many of which, indeed, owe their establishment to his own personal exertions. Mr. Close succeeded
the Rev. C. Jervis, in the perpetual curacy of St. Mary's,
in 1826.

Though the duties of the cure have increased a hun-
dredfold since the days of Sir B. Hicks, no increase has
taken place in the stated value of the incumbancy, which
is still but " forty pounds a-year." The surplice fees, and
other contingencies have, however, borne a fair ratio to
the increase of duties, and the original poverty of the

curacy is thus amply compensated for and proportioned
to the heavy labours entailed upon its possessor. The
value of the living, computed from parliamentary docu-
ments, according to the *Liber Ecclesiasticus*, published
some years ago, amounted to £688 per annum. By the
arrangements consequent upon the passing of the act of
parliament in 1801, for abolishing the tithes and substi-
tuting in lieu thereof allotments in common lands, Cheltenham is for ever relieved from the necessity of paying this
tax, and all property within the parish jurisdiction is consequently tithe-free, a point of no small importance to persons who may be desirous of investing their capital in
either houses or land.

The CHURCHYARD, which has received within its consecrated precincts the successive inhabitants of twenty
generations, comprises nearly an acre of ground, and is
one of the principal thoroughfares leading to the Crescent,
and through the Crescent to the different Spas. Two
highly picturesque avenues, formed of double rows of lime
trees, point out these thoroughfares; and

" Oft when busy crowds retire
    To take their evening rest,"

awaken in the mind associations of monastic seclusion, not
uncongenial to a spot so sacred, while here and there the
deep shadows of the funereal yew tend to strengthen the
transient delusion and harmonize well with the surrounding objects. Near the north entrance of the church is an
ancient stone cross, seven feet high, and in excellent preservation, though supposed to have been erected in the
days of King Edward I., and consequently about five
hundred and fifty years old. The epitaph collector may
here meet with some very curious inscriptions, as well

ludicrous as grave; and in his "Meditations among the Tombs," will be forcibly reminded of Gray's stanzas:

" Yet ev'n these bones from insult to protect,
    Some frail memorial still erected nigh ;
With uncouth rhymes and shapeless sculpture deck'd,
    Implore the passing tribute of a sigh.

Their names, their years, spelt by the unletter'd muse,
    The place of fame and elegy supply :
And many a holy text around she strews,
    To teach the rustic moralist to die."

In consequence of the over-crowded state of the old churchyard, and the increasing population of the town demanding annually increased space for the sepulture of its dead, a NEW BURIAL GROUND or cemetry was resolved upon, and in 1830 a piece of land was purchased by the parish, and a neat little chapel built thereon for the more reverend performance of

NEW BURIAL GROUND.

the funeral service than can, in all weathers, be assured in the open air. The ground comprises an area of ten acres, which is divided into different portions: one space being set apart for vaults, another for plain graves with headstones only, and others again subject to other regulations; so as to preserve something like uniformity of appearance throughout the general arrangement. This cemetry is situated on the left-hand of the High Street, not very far

from the road which turns off to Gloucester. It is shut-in
from the street by lofty iron gates, the path leading from
which to the chapel, has been planted on either hand with
lime and other trees, which form, even already, a suitable
and characteristic approach to this long, last resting place
of the children of men.

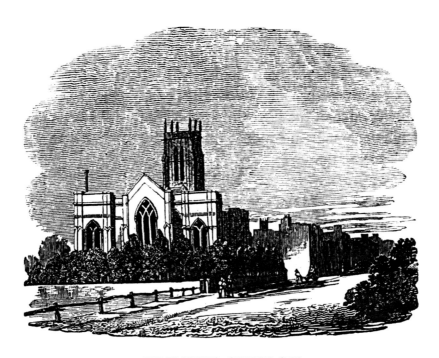

TRINITY CHURCH

is situated on the northern side of the town, at the further
end of Portland Street, and is a chapel of ease to St.
Mary's, in the incumbent of which the right of presentation is vested. The church consists of three ailes and two
spacious galleries, is 74 feet long by 51 broad, and is
capable of containing nine hundred persons; over the
principal entrance, which is on the south side, is a tower,
surmounted by eight light pinnacles. Trinity church, however, is not a favourable specimen of modern ecclesiastical

architecture. The square wings of the front, and the balustrades, or cornice resembling that form, are features quite
abhorrent from the pointed style. The cemetries beneath
the ailes are large, though the external burial ground is
very small and confined. This church was at first intended to have been erected by public subscription, but
these means proving inadequate, Lord Sherborne was induced to undertake its completion at his own expense,
allowing, however, such persons as had originally subscribed, to retain their shares if they so chose; and the
church, or at least the greater portion of it, thus became
the private property of his lordship. The salary of the
officiating minister is secured by a small ground rent on
all the pews, together with some pews appropriated to
him. The proceeds of the cemeteries are devoted to the
repairs of the church, until a fund of £600 shall have been
raised, when the profits will be divided between the incumbent of Cheltenham and Lord Sherborne. The exterior burying ground is the exclusive property of the incumbent of Cheltenham. Seats in this church may be
obtained, either for the week, month, or year, on application
at Lee's Library, 384, High Street, or strangers and occasional visitors are accommodated with sittings on payment of one shilling as they enter. The pews being wholly
private property, this regulation, however in theory unpleasant, is rendered necessary in order to secure to the
proprietors an equitable rate of interest for the money so
invested, and but for which a second church had even
still been wanting in Cheltenham, notwithstanding its great
increase of population. Trinity Church was consecrated
on the 11th of April, 1822, by the Rev. Dr. Ryder, the
then Bishop of Gloucester. The present incumbent is the
Rev. John Browne, who is assisted by a curate. The

hours of divine service on Sundays, are eleven in the morning and three in the afternoon, as at the other churches.

ST. JOHN'S CHURCH

is a plain but neat edifice, situate on the left hand side of Berkeley Street, and capable of affording accommodation to about 900 persons.   It was built in the year 1828, and consecrated the 22nd January, 1829, by Dr. Bethel, then Bishop of Gloucester.   The erection of St. John's church was undertaken by the Rev. W. S. Phillips, at whose almost sole expense it was completed; a few only of his immediate friends taking part with him in the cost thereof. Mr. Phillips, though no longer resident in Cheltenham, is still the incumbent; but the duties are wholly performed by the assistant minister, the Rev. A. Watson, who has lately established schools in connection with his church, for the accommodation of which suitable premises have been erected adjoining the sacred edifice.   Divine service is solemnized at St. John's every Sunday morning at eleven, and afternoon at three o'clock: also, on all holydays at the former hour.   The same regulations are observed here, with respect to the letting and occupying pews, as at Trinity and the other proprietory churches, and which are detailed above. Mr. W. B. Hill, bookseller, 86, High Street, is the appointed agent for letting the sittings in St. John's church.

On the opposite side of the town, a short distance from the Montpellier Pump Room, stands

ST. JAMES'S CHURCH,

or, as it is sometimes called, Suffolk church, from its occupying one corner of Suffolk Square. This building was undertaken by private subscription, or shares, and consecrated for public worship by Dr. Monk, bishop of the diocese, on the 6th of October, 1830. The appointment of the minister is at present vested in three trustees, named by the shareholders, who have allotted four hundred sittings towards defraying all necessary expenses, and the payment of their pastor; ultimately, however, the presentation will lay with the incumbent of the parish. These four hundred sittings, constituting the sole endowment of the church, are mostly let to the residents in the neighbourhood; and occasional visitors, who may be desirous of

K 2

obtaining a seat, are expected to pay one shilling each service, for which tickets will be given them by a person
stationed at the centre door for this purpose. The monies
thus collected form a very important proportion of the
general income, and without which, indeed, the church
could not be kept open, there being neither tithes nor dues
of any kind for the support of the clergyman, other than
the revenue derivable from the sources above mentioned,
and which is secured to him by the deed of consecration.
The church is built in a simple gothic style, and is calculated to contain from fourteen to fifteen hundred persons.
It is furnished with an elegant and powerful organ, made
expressly for it by Mr. Gray, of the New Road, London,
at an expense of little short of £700, and which is considered by the most competent judges as one of the finest
instruments in the county. The original architect was Mr.
E. Jenkins, but the building was finished under the direction and superintendence of J. B. Papworth, Esq., of
London. Persons wishing for sittings in St. James's
church, either for the single Sunday or longer periods,
must apply for them at Mr. Fletcher's, chemist, Montpellier Avenue, where such as are vacant are regularly marked
on the plan. The Rev. J. Balfour is the present minister.
The hours of divine service, on Sunday, are eleven in the
morning, three in the afternoon, and seven in the evening.

ST. PAUL'S, or the FREE CHURCH.

The three churches last described having been altogether erected at the expense of private individuals, or
as joint stock speculations, necessarily partook of an ex-
clusiveness scarcely perhaps recognized by the doctrines of
the Gospel. While every facility was thus afforded to the

wealthy and the affluent, of hearing proclaimed those glad
tidings of salvation which were alike the inheritance of
all mankind, but comparatively little care had hitherto
been manifested to provide for the spiritual instruction of
the poor and the portionless. The parish church, it was
quite obvious, was totally inadequate to the accommodation
of even a tithe of those persons, who, however anxious
they might be of worshiping God according to the forms
of our national establishment, were, from their situation
and circumstances in life, wholly unable to pay for the use
of sittings. To remedy this great evil our excellent pastor,
the Rev. F. Close, proposed the erection of a Free Church,
where the poor might be accommodated as well as the rich;
and to the infinite credit of the town, his proposition was
so cordially received and supported that, in a very short
time, the sum of three thousand five hundred pounds was
raised by voluntary contributions alone, in order to carry it
into effect. To the sums thus obtained, the Government
Commissioners for building churches added three thousand
pounds; and a plot of ground on the north side of the
town, a little beyond Henrietta Street, was presented by
the late Joseph Pitt, Esq. Under these favourable auspices
the undertaking was very soon completed, and on the 12th
of July, 1831, the Free Church was consecrated for divine
worship by the Bishop of Gloucester, since which time
public service has been regularly performed there every
Sunday at the usual hours. The building itself is roomy
and commodious, having galleries, and an organ, presented
to the congregation by their former pastor, the Rev. Sir
Henry Thompson. The right of presentation is vested
in the perpetual curate of St. Mary's, and the maintenance and expenses of the church are chargeable upon the
parish, to which, consequently, St. Paul's must be consi-

dered as a chapel of ease.   It is capable of holding 1600
persons.   The present minister is the Rev. J. H. Sharwood.

CHRIST CHURCH,

the most recently erected of the proprietory churches of the
parish, is also the largest and the most beautiful in its
architectural appearance.   It is conspicuously situated on
the Alstone slope of Bays Hill, at the end of Lansdown
Terrace, and immediately fronting the new road recently
opened into the Queen's Road.   It was consecrated to
divine worship by Dr. Monk, the bishop of the diocese,
on the 26th of January, 1840, when the Rev. C. E. Ken-
naway accepted the incumbancy, which, however, he re-
signed at the expiration of two years; and the present
incumbent, the Rev. A. Boyd, was appointed his successor, January, 1842. The presentation is vested in three

trustees, chosen by the proprietors, for a period of forty years, when it lapses to the mother church. The present trustees are the Rev. F. Close, the Rev. Carus Wilson, and Joseph Wilkinson, Esq.

Christ Church is calculated to accommodate two thousand persons, and measures one hundred and thirty feet in length, by one hundred and seven in breadth, taken through the transepts, which are themselves very large. Its western tower is universally and justly admired, being built and decorated in the elaborated architectural styles of the 13th and 14th centuries, having elegant pinnacles rising from the corners. The total height of this tower to the apex of the pinnacles is 174 feet. The church is pewed throughout, and the pulpit is of stone beautifully carved. The organ, which is placed in the tower, was built by Messrs. Hill & Co., of London, and is considered a very fine instrument. The architect of this noble edifice was R. W. Jearrad, Esq., who also personally superintended its erection. The total cost of the building and interior fittings amounted to upwards of eighteen thousand pounds, which was raised in hundred pound shares, to each of which seven sittings were allotted in the church; on all these an annual ground rent of five shillings each is chargeable, which, with the proceeds of certain pews assigned to the incumbent, constitutes the endowment. The hours of service on Sundays are 11 a.m., and 3½ p.m. The agent for Christ church is Mr. H. Davies, Montpellier Library, to whom all applications for sittings, by the day, month, or longer period, should be made. The prices per sitting vary according to their position in the church—those in the middle aisle and along the front of the gallery being a guinea and a half per annum, and those in the side aisles and transepts ranging from fifteen to twenty-eight shillings each. Strangers are accommodated with occasional sittings on purchase of tickets at the entrance, which are charged one shilling each, as at the other proprietary churches of the town.

ST. PHILIP'S CHURCH,

on the confines of Leckhampton parish, within which it is situated, is yet, from its locality—a short distance beyond Suffolk Square—very properly considered as pertaining to Cheltenham. It was erected in 1839-40, for the purpose of supplying the populous districts of the Bath road with religious instruction—the funds for its erection being raised partly by donations and partly by proprietary shares. The building, which was designed by Mr. Shellard, is neat in its external appearance, and has a very pretty little tower, eighty-six feet in height, rising above the eastern entrance. The interior is eighty-five feet in length by forty-one in breadth, and is capable of accommodating eight hundred and fifty persons. There are three hundred and fifty sittings free, one hundred and eighty apportioned to the proprietary, the remaining three hundred and twenty forming the endowment. St. Philip's church, and the burial ground by which it is surrounded, were consecrated by Dr. Monk, bishop of Gloucester, on the 1st of May, 1840. The present incumbent is the Rev. J. E. Riddle. The hours of divine service, on Sundays, are the same as those of the other churches—11 a.m. and 3 p.m. The agent for letting the pews is Mr. Lapidge, Suffolk Parade.

Having thus given an account of the various churches, we now turn to the consideration of the principal dissenting places of worship in the town, and shall commence with a brief notice of

CHELTENHAM CHAPEL,

which is a neat building, occupying the south-eastern side of St. George's Square, surrounded by a court yard communicating with the High Street and St. George's Place. It was erected under the auspices of the Rev. Rowland Hill, and opened for religious service in August, 1809. It has a gallery along the front and two sides, and is provided with a good organ. The pews immediately under the gallery are, properly speaking, the only private seats in the chapel; those which occupy the centre being all of them open. Though denominated a congregation of Protestant dissenters, there appears little in its forms of worship differing from the generality of chapels of ease connected with the established church; the authorized liturgy being used both at morning and evening service, and it being required by the deed of enrolment, that the minister should always be a regularly ordained clergyman. Like most dissenting places of worship, it was originally built by public contributions, and is still supported by the subscriptions of its stated congregation, and the voluntary donations of occasional visitors. The present minister is the Rev. J. Brown, who has held the appointment ever since the chapel was first opened. There is a Sunday school connected with this chapel.

WESLEYAN METHODIST CHAPELS.

The Wesleyan Methodists, the most numerous and influential of all the denominations of dissenters, have had places of public worship in Cheltenham for nearly half a century; and, at the present time, are possessed of two chapels built originally by themselves, and subject to the general regulations of the connection in respect to such edifices, being vested in trustees for the use of the society, and duly enrolled in Chancery. The former are considered responsible for all secular matters of administration and management, while to the Methodist Conference pertain all ecclesiastical authority, and the appointment of the ministers, who are usually changed every two or three years. There are two travelling preachers appointed to the Cheltenham circuit, and one supernumerary. Besides which there are a number of lay or local preachers, members of the society, who supply the pulpits of several small chapels in the surrounding villages; and, occasionally, also officiate for the regular preachers, when the latter undertake the ministerial duties of the rural districts.

The principal Methodist Chapel is in St. George's Street, and was erected in 1838-9, at a cost of three thousand pounds. It was opened in the latter year—the congregation which had, for the previous twenty-seven years, occupied Ebenezer chapel, in King Street, being then removed to the new and more commodious edifice.

Wesley Chapel is, exteriorly, a plain square building, having, however, a deep portico, supported by four pillars in front. The interior, which is estimated to accommodate about a thousand persons, is exceedingly neat, and pewed throughout, having galleries

WESLEY CHAPEL.

disproportionably large along the front and three sides, and one for the organ and singers immediately behind the pulpit. The organ is generally considered a very good one for its size, and cost £350. There are very spacious rooms beneath the chapel, principally used as Sunday schools. The hours of Sabbath-day service are—morning, at eleven; and evening, at half-past six. There is also service every Tuesday evening at seven. The Missionary and other religious societies connected with the Methodist body celebrate their anniversaries in Wesley chapel.

BETHESDA CHAPEL, Great Norwood Street, a short distance beyond Suffolk Square, is a small place of worship, belonging to the Wesleyan Methodists, in which divine service is regularly performed thrice every Sunday at the customary hours.

BAPTISTS' CHAPELS.

The Baptists were among the first dissenters of whom we find any mention made, in connection with the history of the rise and progress of Cheltenham; a congregation of this body having been formed here as early as 1700. For the use of this congregation a small chapel was erected and opened in the following year. This, in course of time, being found too confined for the accommodation of its increasing numbers, was pulled down, and in the year 1820-21 the present BETHEL CHAPEL built upon its scite, at a cost of £1450. The dimensions of the original building were thirty-eight feet long by twenty feet broad: those of the present one fifty-two feet by thirty-five. It is situated opposite the east corner of St. James's Square, about a hundred yards from the Roman Catholic chapel. About ten years ago a disagreement sprang up among the members of the congregation, respecting some matters of internal regulation or government, and a schism thereupon took place, which ended in the withdrawal of the then minister, a Rev. Mr. Smith, and a great number of the congregation, who were attached to his ministrations. These established an independent place of worship in Regent Street, which they denominated SALEM CHAPEL, where, for many years, the Rev. Mr. Smith fulfilled the duties of pastor; and, on his acceptance of another appointment near London, was, in 1842, succeeded by the present minister. In a very few years after Mr. Smith's secession, a second division arose among the congregation of Bethel, and a second off-set was the consequence; a large proportion of the number following the retiring preacher, a Mr. Leader, who established himself, in 1840, in EBENEZER CHAPEL, King Street, formerly occupied by the Methodists, by whom it was vacated on the erection of Wesley chapel, to which they removed as above stated. At each of these chapels divine service is performed every Sunday morning, afternoon, and evening; and there are, likewise, other services connected with the respective societies at other times.

PORTLAND CHAPEL

was built in 1816, at the sole expense of Robert Capper, Esq., one of the sitting magistrates of the town, and then resident at Marle Hill. Three years after its erection, Mr. Capper generously presented it to the trustees of the late Countess of Huntingdon, who have from time to time supplied it with ministers from their own particular connexion. The chapel, which is situated at the further end of North Place, at its junction with Portland Street, is rather a handsome building, having galleries and a good organ, and is estimated to contain from eight to nine hundred persons. Portions of the Liturgy of the Established Church are read at both the morning and evening services every Sunday. It has a Sunday school attached, belonging to its own congregation, and the day-school of the " Cheltenham Protestant Union " is kept in the rooms beneath the chapel.

HIGHBURY CHAPEL.

This place of worship was originally built for the Rev. Mr. Snow, a seceder from the Church of England, and who had previously officiated at Portland chapel. It is vested in public trust for the use of the Independents or Congregationalists, and divine service is performed here twice every Sunday, according to the tenets and forms of worship peculiar to that denomination. It has, hitherto,

been supplied with a succession of ministers, chosen by
the members and trustees of the chapel. The building is
extremely neat, and light and airy in its internal appearance. Both the galleries and the body are pewed off, and
a considerable number of free seats are ranged near the
entrance, for the accommodation of the poorer members
of the congregation. A Sunday school is attached to the
chapel, suitable buildings having been recently erected for
its reception.

THE QUAKERS' MEETING HOUSE.

The Quakers appear to have been the first noncon-
formists who organised a congregation in Cheltenham,
having built a chapel in the town so early as 1660. This
was in Manchester Walk, St. George's Place, in which
building the members of this community continued to
worship, according to their own peculiar forms, until 1835,
when a much larger edifice was built, a few yards distant
from the original chapel, which was, on the opening of
the new structure, sold. The latter presents an exceedingly plain, yet neat, exterior, and is capable of containing
about three hundred persons; and it is here that the
Society of Friends now hold their meetings for public
worship.

THE ROMAN CATHOLIC CHAPEL

stands at the corner of Somerset Place, having the residence of the officiating clergyman immediately adjoining. It was first opened for divine service in 1810, the
cost of its erection having been defrayed by voluntary
subscription; and it is still indebted to a continuance of
the same liberality for its support, the weekly contributions which are received at the doors being the chief de-

pendence of the pastor. The exterior of the building is utterly devoid of decoration, but a light and elegant interior compensates for the lack of ornament without. It has a commodious gallery; and over the altar is a painting of "The Last Supper," copied from one by Raphael at the Vatican. The chapel is capable of containing about five hundred persons, and it is generally very well attended. The hours of full service are eleven o'clock on Sundays and holidays; and mass is celebrated every morning throughout the year at nine o'clock. There is a school attached for educating the children of poor Catholics.

THE UNITARIAN CHAPEL

is in Manchester Walk, being the building originally occupied by the Quakers, and who having disposed of it on the erection of their larger place of worship, hard by, it passed into private hands, and was let to the society now tenanting the premises, in the year 1835; a short time previous to which the first Unitarian congregation was organized in Cheltenham. The hours of public service, on Sundays, are eleven o'clock in the morning and seven in the evening. There is a Sunday school attached to the chapel. The chapel is capable of accommodating from one hundred and fifty to two hundred persons. A building capable of containing double that number is in course of erection at the Crescent end of the Old Well Walk, immediately behind Royal Well Terrace. The estimated cost of this new chapel is £1500. It is expected to be completed in 1844.

THE JEWS' SYNAGOGUE

is a small building at the end of St. George's Terrace, and immediately opposite the entrance to the Infants'

School. It was built eight or ten years ago, previous to which time the descendants of Abraham worshipped the God of their fathers in an apartment appropriated to that purpose in Manchester Place.

———

In addition to the places of religious worship, above particularized, there are a number of small chapels or meeting houses of minor note and importance, in different parts of the town, being, for the most part, off-sets from some one or other of those already mentioned; but as these little communities rarely enjoy more than an ephemeral existence, and prefer no claims to the notice of the stranger, we shall not, at present, detain him with even an enumeration of them in our pages.

CHAPTER IX.

BENEVOLENT AND CHARITABLE INSTITUTIONS.

*General Hospital and Dispensary—Female Orphan Asylum—Provident and
Clothing Institution—Cobourg Society—Dispensary for the Diseases
of Women and Children—Loan Fund—Servants' Home—Religious
Societies—Pates' Alms Houses—National Schools—Infant Schools—
Protestant Union Schools—Sunday Schools, &c.*

THE great number of charitable institutions which, within
the last forty years, have been established in this country,
will serve for ever to characterize the nineteenth century,
in Britain, as emphatically the century of public benevolence.

The world had long known, in theory at least, the
value of union and co-operation in all important undertakings connected with its multiform schemes of aggran-
dizement and conquest; but it was reserved for the present generation to discover their great importance, when
directed to objects of peace and philanthropy. Time has
been, indeed, when the accumulated wealth of a single
individual was not unfrequently devoted to the founding
and endowment of schools, hospitals, and colleges, with a
munificence that seems to contemn the puny efforts of
modern liberality; but it has been the ill fortune of most
of the places thus instituted, to have soon fallen to decay,

L

or else to have remained in the rear of advancing civiliza-
tion, converted into unmeaning monuments of charities
long since extinct, and useless to all save a few well-paid
sinecurists. The reason of all this is obvious. The founder
alone felt any real interest in the welfare of such establishments; there was no appeal to, no union of, the sympa-
thies of his fellow men; and when the one prompting
spirit was removed by death, there remained no second to
fill up the void: the heir to his estates inherited not his
virtues. In our own days benevolence pursues a different
plan, and one that promises to be more permanent, as
well as more extensive in its effects. The support and co-
operation of the many are sought for and secured; hence
an interest is created in the breasts of thousands, who
otherwise would have been strangers to the glow of
Christian sympathy. The spirit of modern philanthropy
claims kindred with the living feelings and affections of
mankind, and aims rather to afford present and efficient
relief, than to merit, by any ostentatious liberality, the
praises of future generations.

Many of the benevolent institutions of our own times
have been established, and are still wholly supported, by
the adopters of peculiar creeds and the members of particular denominations of Christians; but there are others
which, recognizing neither sect nor party, appeal directly
to those principles of universal charity inherent in the
human mind, and which, however much in abeyance for a
season, are never entirely extinct. Such are the principles
upon which has been founded the

GENERAL HOSPITAL AND DISPENSARY,

which is situated in the High Street, nearly opposite St.
George's Square, having a gravelled court yard in front,

and which was established upon its present broad basis in 1839. A Dispensary and Casualty Hospital had existed for many years previously, having been instituted in 1813; but their plans and objects proved wholly insufficient for the increasing wants of a population which had mightily outgrown its first estate. A generous effort was, consequently, made in 1838-9 to extend the benefits of the institution, by embracing a more enlarged sphere of benevolence, and combining permanent wards for the reception of in-patients, with the system of out-door relief originally afforded. Adequate funds having been raised by donations and public collections, the present buildings were purchased and furnished as a General Hospital. Between forty and fifty beds are now made up in the establishment for the reception of the more serious cases of disease and accident; and there are capabilities in the premises for the erection of about thirty more, whenever the exigencies of the town shall require, and the funds, at the disposal of the managers, shall enable such additional number to be fitted up. Some idea of the extensive operations of this benevolent institution may be formed from the fact that the average annual number of out-patients relieved is about five thousand, and that of the in-patients three hundred. Among the latter there are always many very serious cases, requiring skilful medical treatment, or the performance of surgical operations, such as could rarely have been successfully accomplished at the poor homes of the patients themselves.

The affairs of the Hospital are conducted by a board or committee of management, consisting of eighteen governors, who meet every Monday to attend to and direct the general business of the institution. There are also three physicians and two surgeons attached to the Hospital department, and a like number of each to that of the Dispensary: and besides all these, which are honorary appointments, there are a resident house-surgeon and other officers, such as are usually connected with similar establishments.

The benefits conferred upon the town by this establishment are, we rejoice to say, not unappreciated by the respectable inhabitants, most of whom contribute to its support. All subscribers of one guinea a-year and upwards have the privilege of recommending patients for admission, and proper letters for this purpose can at any time be obtained, on application to the house apothecary, at No. 318, High Street. Within late years a Museum of Natural History has been added to the establishment, and many very curious and valuable specimens, connected with the study of medical science, have been already collected; indeed, this department promises ere long to be one of considerable importance.

THE FEMALE ORPHAN ASYLUM,

Winchcomb Street, originally a school of industry, was instituted in 1806 by the late Queen Charlotte, for the education and maintenance of female children of the poor, a preference being given to such as were orphans; to the admission of whom alone it has now for several years been wholly confined. The present building was erected in 1833-4, from designs of R. Stokes, Esq.; the Bishop of Gloucester laying the foundation stone, August 30 in the former year. The main building, which is in imitation of the gothic or tudor order of architecture, is nearly seventy feet long; and the name of the Institution is inscribed along the parapet in grotesque gothic characters. The primary objects aimed at by the Cheltenham Female Orphan Asylum, are the inculcation of correct moral and religious

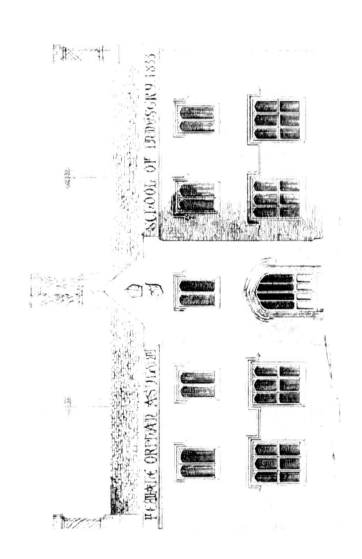

SCHOOL OF LINDESAY 1833

principles into the minds of the children; and, by instruct-
ing them in every description of household labour, to
qualify them for filling their respective stations in life,
with credit to themselves and satisfaction to their em-
ployers. No child is admitted under the age of eight, nor
above the age of ten, nor retained there after the age of
fifteen, unless such continuance be specially approved of
by the committee of management; and when a child leaves
the asylum she is entitled to an outfit, provided her conduct has been such as to merit approval. All applications
from persons desirous of taking an orphan from the asylum
must be made in writing to the committee of superintendence, and the nature of the proposed situation specified.
When any vacancies occur among the inmates they are
filled up by election at the half-yearly meetings, which take
place in the spring and autumn; and a child to become a
candidate must be recommened either by a governor or
annual subscriber. The average number of children in the
asylum is about thirty. It is open to the public every
Tuesday and Friday, from one till four o'clock. The Lord
Bishop of Gloucester is the patron, and Lady Sherborne
the patroness of the institution.

THE PROVIDENT CLOTHING INSTITUTION

is another benevolent society, which has now been for
some time in useful and active operation. Its objects are
to furnish the poor with clothing at the very lowest possible prices—not always insisting upon such prices being
according to the absolute cost of the articles furnished—
any differences being made good by the subscriptions and
donations of its benevolent supporters. The office of the
institution is at No. 300, High Street.

THE COBOURG SOCIETY

was founded by the late Rev. C. Jervis, for the purpose of affording relief to poor women during the time of their confinement. This relief consists in supplies of clothing and child-bed linen, which are lent during the period in question, and which are returned to the Society's stores as soon as the objects of such grants have sufficiently recovered to be again enabled to attend to the domestic duties entailed upon them as wives and mothers. The affairs of the Society are managed by a committee of ladies, a treasurer, two secretaries, and a storekeeper. Its name is the consequence of its having been instituted to commemorate the lamented death of the late Princess Charlotte of Wales and Saxe Cobourg, upon the day of whose funeral its benevolent founder formally commenced its proceedings. The present patroness is the Right Hon. Lady Sherborne. The office of the society is at No. 300, High Street.

THE DISPENSARY FOR THE DISEASES OF WOMEN AND CHILDREN, St. George's Street, is a kindred charitable institution, having for its most immediate object the administration of medical and surgical assistance to poor Lying-in Women, who, from their circumstances in life, might be unable to obtain such aid at their own charge. The society is managed by a medical and ladies' committee, assisted by the usual officers.

CHELTENHAM LOAN FUND,

a society formed in 1835, for the benevolent purpose of advancing small sums of money to indigent tradesmen and the labouring classes generally, being properly recommended as fit objects for such assistance. The sums so lent are required to be repaid by weekly or other instalments —no interest being charged thereon. The capital whence these advances are made, has been created by subscription and donations, and is administered by a committee of gentlemen, who also manage the affairs of the society. The office of the Cheltenham Loan Fund is at 300, High Street.

THE SERVANTS' HOME,

Vernon House, at the Cambray end of the Bath road, is an institution established a few year ago by several kind and benevolent ladies with a view of affording, at all times, an asylum for respectable female servants out of place, and who are permitted, at a very trifling expense, to continue here until suited with situations. As none are admitted into this house whose characters will not bear a strict investigation, the institution offers to families requiring servants, an eligible medium for supplying one of the most difficult of all domestic wants. The affairs of the Home are managed by a committee of ladies; and there are two matrons resident on the premises, to whom reference can always be had.

The BIBLE, MISSIONARY, as well as most of the other religious societies throughout the country, have auxiliary branches in Cheltenham, all of which are liberally contributed to by the residents of the place. Their public and anniversary meetings are mostly held in the Philosophical Institution. As, however, it would occupy too large a portion of our work to enter upon the details of all these institutions, we must content ourselves with merely noticing their existence. Such persons as feel an interest in their welfare and success, will find no difficulty in ob-

taining every information they may require respecting them
from the clergy of the establishment resident in the
town; or from the dissenting ministers, for such of them
as may be connected with their own particular societies
and congregations.

PATE'S CHARITIES.

The present state of these charities affords a happy
illustration to the remarks made at the commencement
of the present chapter—namely, that unless the sym-
pathies of the living be awakened, and called in to the
assistance and support of our benevolent institutions,
these will generally be found to fall rapidly into disuetude
and decay; and foundations, the boast and glory of one
generation, thus not unfrequently become worse than useless to the next, Motives of interest will, indeed, be
always found sufficiently powerful to preserve them from
absolute extinction, or being forfeited for want of a formal
recognition of their existence; but the skeleton of charity
which survives, is destitute of all the essential and efficient principles of vitality.

In the year 1586, Richard Pate, of Minsterworth,
and recorder of Gloucester, bequeathed several plots of
ground in and around Cheltenham, the annual rents of
which then amounted to £73. 19s. 4d., for the endowment
of a free grammar school, and an alms house or hospital
for six poor people; and the more effectually to secure
the fulfilment of his benevolent intentions, placed the management and administration of the bequest in the president and seven seniors of Corpus-Christi college, Oxford,
to whom, indeed, one-fourth of the net produce of the
estates in question was assigned. Within the last hundred years, the value of the property forming this endow-

ment has increased in a surprising degree, and it is calculated that the annual receipts now amount to at least
£600. The use of this money is enjoyed by the college
trustees, who, acting upon the letter rather than the
spirit of the founder's intentions, have, by an apathy too
common in similar cases, reduced these charities to a state
of comparative abeyance. In 1816 the parish of Cheltenham commenced proceedings in Chancery against the
principal and masters of Corpus Christi, in order to com-
pel them to give to the foresaid school and alms house
the full benefit of the great increase which had taken place
in the income of the estates. Hitherto, however, little
or no progress has been made towards effecting so important and desirable a restoration.

In the grant of Richard Pate, the ALMS HOUSE "for six
poor people, whereof two at the least shall be poor
women," is directed "to be for ever called and named by
the title of the Hospital or Alms House of the indivisible Trinity." The provision made for the inmates,
besides their lodging and a yearly allowance of seven
yards of black frieze to the men and five to the women,
consisted of 1s. per week to each, with "fourpence
apiece to be delivered to them, over and besides their
week's wages, at every of the feasts of All Saints, Christ-
mas, Easter, and Pentecost, yearly." The qualification
for admission required that the candidate should "be of
the age of three-score years at the least, or have some
notable impotency or disease, not like to be cured, being
not infectious, and should also be able to rehearse without
book, and by memory, the Lord's prayer, the articles of
our belief, and the ten commandments of God;" and that
they should be born within the parishes of Cheltenham or
Leigh. The right of nominating persons thus qualified

was granted by the founder to "Susan Brooke, and the heirs of her body lawfully begotten: or for default of such issue, by three of the next of kindred to the said Richard Pate, or by two of those three for the time being, from time to time for ever. Provided that John Pate, of Charleton, nor any descending from him, be any of those three, for his ingratitude to the hospital." What the said John Pate, of Charleton, had done, to have incurred the heavy displeasure of the benevolent Richard, we are no where informed; but, "certes," it must have been some very signal act of ingratitude. In the present day the right of electing the pensioners is exercised by the church-wardens. The sum of £18 was assigned by the will of the founder to the maintenance of these alms houses; a sum ample and liberal at the period of their foundation. They are situated in Albion Street.

From the "Hospital of the Holy and Indivisible Trinity," we turn to another and more important endowment of Richard Pate's,

THE FREE GRAMMAR SCHOOL,

intended for the education of " fifty scholars at the least," who were to be instructed in Greek, Latin, or English grammar. Each of these scholars was required, on his first admission, to pay four pence, if resident in the parish of Cheltenham, and eight pence if in any other parish; " with which money the schoolmaster, with the consent and appointment of the visitors, shall buy and provide such Latin and Greek books as shall be most necessary for the public use of the said scholars, *to be tied fast with little chains of iron for that purpose,* in some convenient place in the said school." Such fees, however, when a sufficient number of books had been provided, " the schoolmaster for the time being was to receive to his own use." The appointment of the master and usher was vested in Corpus Christi College, at which place Richard Pate informs us he had himself "been brought up here-tofore in good letters." The yearly salary of the master, who is required "to be a master of arts in degree, and of the age of thirty years at least," was originally fixed at £16, and that of the usher at £4, though we believe a more liberal sum is now allowed by the college, the amount of the revenue derived from the estates appointed to the support of the school having surprisingly increased since "the eight and twentieth year of the reign of our Sovereign Lady Elizabeth." In the year 1682, George Townsend, Esq., of Lincoln's Inn, left by will £8 a-year towards the maintenance of eight scholars, being youths of the county, at Pembroke College, Oxford, two of whom were to be chosen from the Free Grammar School of Cheltenham. These exhibitions are now worth £60 per annum. There are also four livings or donatives, to which they are exclusively eligible, viz.:

Colnbrook .... (Donative) .... Bucks.
Stifford .... (Rectory)............. Essex.
Thurrock Greys.. ...... (Vicarage) .... Essex.
Uxbridge .... (Donative) .... Middlesex.

The school house is an old-fashioned building on the right hand side of the High Street, a few minutes' walk below the Arcade.

———

NATIONAL SCHOOL.

This institution is situated in the Bath road, within a short distance of the Montpellier Baths. The building itself is very neat and convenient, as well as perfectly adapted for the purposes to which it is appropriated. The system of instruction introduced by the late Dr. Bell,* and now so generally adopted throughout a great part of the world, was first applied to the education of the children of the poor of Cheltenham in the year 1816; when a committee was formed for the purpose of carrying the benevolent design more fully into effect; and the present school house, which was opened Jan. 6, 1817, is a consequence of their exertions. As most persons are now acquainted with the plan upon which these institutions are conducted, and as the Cheltenham National School differs in no respect from similar establishments in other parts of the kingdom, it will not be necessary for us here to enter upon any detailed examination of its constitution and government; we may, however, just observe that it is wholly supported by public subscriptions and donations, and the produce of an annual collection made at the different churches in the town. Besides the parent institution here spoken of, there are two important branch schools—one in connection with St. Paul's church, and the other with that of Trinity. The number of children under instruction in each of these establishments, in 1842, including the Sunday scholars, were

In the Bath Road School 250

Trinity Church School 338

St. Paul's School 449

Total 1037

* Dr. Bell was a resident at Cheltenham for many years before his death, which took place at Lindsay Cottage (now called Wolseley Villa) on the 27th of January, 1832. His remains were honoured with a public funeral in Westminster Abbey, on the 10th of the following month.

A Day and Sunday School upon the National plan of instruction has also lately been established in connection with St. John's church.

These Schools are at all times open to the inspection of visitors friendly to the Christian education of the rising generation; and every information respecting their state and management may be obtained from the respective officers, or from any of the clergy of the town, most of whom take a warm interest in their prosperity.

INFANT SCHOOLS.

Until within the last few years any attempt to educate the mere infant would have been deemed, to say the least of it, wild and visionary; but experience has now fully proved that theory, however specious, is not always to be relied upon for the conclusions at which it arrives. Indeed, the sight of institutions like those at present under notice, cannot fail of convincing the most prejudiced advocates of the time-enough systems of old, that there is literally *no* time to be lost in cultivating the dawning affections of the young, and in forming the mind to habits of virtue. The poor, from their station in life, are generally too much occupied in providing for the bodily wants of their families, to allow of their devoting much time to the moral training and intellectual cultivation of their children, who are consequently often suffered to grow up in vice and ignorance. To correct this serious evil the establishment of Infant Schools was proposed, in order to provide a nursery for the offspring of those who were themselves unable to do so. The first institution of this description was, we believe, attempted at Liverpool, and proved so successful that most of the populous towns in England soon followed the example thus set them, and

among others the town of Cheltenham. Under the auspices
of the Rev. F. Close, whose works of benevolence we have
already in more than one instance had occasion to advert
to, the Infant School was commenced by Mr. Wilderspin, the founder of the system, in 1825, in the adjoining
hamlet of Alstone, where a branch still remains. The
exertions of our worthy pastor were not confined to the
mere establishment of the institution, but were continued
until he had raised by public subscriptions and donations a sum of money adequate to defray the expenses of
building the present school-room, which is a particularly
neat and commodious edifice, situated immediately at the
back of the Crescent, and very near St. James's Square.
It was opened in 1828. There is also a play-ground attached, full of swings and other gymnastic erections, for
the use of the juvenile inmates. Children are admitted
so early as the age of two years, and there are between
two and three hundred at present under instruction. We
believe the Cheltenham school is the largest of the kind
in the kingdom. The stranger will be highly gratified by
a visit to this academy of infant scholars.

Besides the central school in St. James's Square, and the
Alstone branch, there have been since established the
Waterloo school, on the Tewkesbury road; the Naunton
school, in Exmouth Street; and the Fairview school, in
Sherborne Street. The total average number of children
on the books of the five schools exceeds a thousand.

PROTESTANT UNION SCHOOL.

This school is held in the large room beneath the
Countess of Huntingdon's chapel, in North Place, and
is intended principally for the education of the children
of poor persons connected with the congregations of the

different dissenting chapels in the town, though nothing like exclusion or sectarianism is observed in its direction and management. The plan of instruction comprehends reading, writing, and the rules of common arithmetic. The children each pay one penny per week, towards the expenses of stationery, books, &c. The salary of the master, and the other unavoidable expenses, are defrayed by annual subscriptions and voluntary contributions. There are generally from two to three hundred children receiving instruction in this school.

A GIRLS' SCHOOL, conducted upon like principles, and under the same auspices, direction, and management, has been lately established, and a building erected especially for its accommodation in St. George's Street.

THE SUNDAY SCHOOLS in Cheltenham are numerous and well conducted. The principal ones are those in connection with the national schools already described; and there are likewise others attached to the parish church, to Christ church, and to St. John's, and at the Naunton and Waterloo school rooms. In the four last named there were between 500 and 600 children under instruction in 1842. These schools all regularly attend divine worship at one or other of the churches every Sunday. At the different dissenting chapels there are also similar institutions for the education of the children of the poor of their respective congregations.

CHAPTER X.

PUBLIC OFFICES AND COMPANIES.

The Post Office—Stamp Office—Markets and Fairs—Gloucester and Birmingham and Cheltenham and Great Western Railways—Gas Company—Cheltenham Water Works' Company—Sewers' Company Banks—Savings' Bank.

ONE of the places first enquired for by strangers, on their arrival in Cheltenham, is

THE POST OFFICE.

This is situated on the left-hand side of Clarence Street, a few doors from Crescent Place—occupying premises erected especially for its reception. It is open throughout the day for the transaction of business, and throughout the greater part of the night also—most of the mails arriving in and departing from the town between ten p.m. and six a.m.

The London down mails arrive in Cheltenham between three and four o'clock in the morning, and the up mails leave between eleven and twelve at night. Those from Birmingham and the North of England, with Ireland, North Wales, and Scotland, arrive at three and half-past five in the morning; and depart, the first mail at seven, and the second at a quarter before nine p.m. The former conveys all letters intended for transmission by the North

Midland railways to Derbyshire, Yorkshire, &c.—the latter for those of Liverpool and the northern counties generally, Ireland, Scotland, &c. The Post Office letter-box closes one hour before the departure of each of these mails, but even during this time, which is occupied in making up the respective bags, letters may still be posted on payment of a penny each for the first half hour, and twopence for the second.

There are two general deliveries through the town daily, the one between eight and nine in the morning, the other between four and five in the afternoon. The latter is mostly for letters brought in by the London day mail, and for such as may be posted for the town itself subsequent to the eight o'clock delivery. Letters are given out to parties applying for them, at the office window, any time during the day.

The Money Order Office for the issue and payment of money orders for sums not exceeding £5, is open from 10 to half-past 3 o'clock daily, Sundays excepted.

There are half a dozen BRANCH RECEIVING HOUSES in different parts of the town, where letters may be posted as at the general office, to which they are officially dispatched three times a day, namely, at 3. 30. for the first north mail and the local afternoon delivery—7. 30. for the second north mail, Ireland, Scotland, &c.—and 10 p.m. for London and all places in the route and beyond.

The Postmaster is Mr. J. Nicholson, to whom all communications relating to the business of this department should be addressed.

———

THE GOVERNMENT STAMP OFFICE

is in Winchcomb Street, No. 38; and is open daily from ten o'clock to four for the sale of every description of

M

stamps; and for the transaction of other business connected with the collection of this important branch of the public revenue. The sub-distributor of stamps for the Cheltenham district is Mr. Spinney.

PUBLIC MARKET.

The Market Place, which was formerly situated on the left hand side of the High Street, was removed to the more eligible site which it now occupies, in the year 1822; the Right Honourable Lord Sherborne, who was then lord of the manor, having erected the present roomy and commodious market house, at the upper end of the Arcade, for the greater convenience and accommodation of the town. The entrance to the Arcade is a few paces be-

THE MARKET ARCADE.

low the Town Clock, and immediately opposite St. Mary's church. Its façade of three arches, in no way remarkable for beauty or appropriateness of architectural design, serves, notwithstanding, to relieve the monotonous appearance of the long line of irregular shop fronts with which it ranges, and more readily arrests the stranger's attention than would a building corresponding to the houses above and below it, or even a space altogether open. Few markets are better supplied with every description of provision; and from the abundance regularly poured in from the neighbouring villages, the prices of the necessaries of life are always extremely moderate, notwithstanding the increase of population, and the consequently increased consumption. The principal market is on Thursdays, though there is no lack of every delicacy in season on the other days of the week.

FAIRS are held in Cheltenham on the second Thursday in April, Holy Thursday, the 5th of August, the second Thursday in September, the third Thursday in December, and the Thursday preceding and following Old Michaelmas-day. The last two are statute-fairs, or, as they are called in the common parlance of Gloucestershire, "mops."

RAILWAYS.

Cheltenham has possessed the advantages of railway communication, either wholly or in part, ever since 1841, when the Gloucester and Birmingham line was completed. This connected our town with the main stream of communication running up to London on the one hand, and down to Liverpool on the other; and, by means of the several other lines branching out of this stream, with the extensive and populous districts of the central and northern counties of England. Another railway, proceeding from Cheltenham to Gloucester, and thence up the valley of Rodborogh, *viá* Stroud and Cirencester, to a junction with the Great Western line at Swindon, is already far advanced, and will, when finished, afford great additional facilities of access to those at present enjoyed. This latter is called the CHELTENHAM AND GREAT WESTERN UNION RAILWAY. The portion from Swindon to Cirencester has been for some time in full operation, and coaches constantly run from Cheltenham to meet the various up and down trains which proceed to and from the **Great Western** line, with which this branch is in immediate connexion.

THE GLOUCESTER AND BIRMINGHAM RAILWAY STATION.

The Cheltenham Station of the Gloucester and Birmingham Railway is situated at the junction of the Queen's with the old Gloucester roads, and is distant about a mile and a half from the centre of the High Street. The principal building consists of the Company's booking and other offices, and the refreshment and waiting rooms for the reception and general accommodation of the public. These all open immediately on to the railway, which passes at a level much lower than that of the carriage roads, and leading down to which are several broad flights of steps, descending from the booking office platforms. Fronting the entrance gates, a neat colonnade is thrown out from the building, under cover of which the carriages and other vehicles set down their passengers—to the right is a range of sheds, beneath which the omnibuses are drawn up while waiting the arrival of the trains—and extending a considerable distance to the left are offices and warehouses appropriated to the goods and traffic of the line. In the

distance, beyond these warehouses, the rail-road shows
itself proceeding beneath the Lansdown bridge, as shown
in the engraving given above.

The line passing immediately under the Gloucester
road may be seen for a very considerable portion of its extension north-
ward from the
right hand side
of the way; &,
looking over
the wall on the
left, its course
may be fol-
lowed beneath
the iron bridge
which crosses
the line, form-

THE RAILWAY STATION.

ing a covered way from the station to the platform, upon
which the passengers *from* Gloucester, and *to* Birmingham,
assemble—the " down trains " discharging their traffic on
the broad pavement under the embankment wall, immediately above which the station and offices of the company
are situated. The arrangements and disposition of these
buildings, as well as of all the working departments of the
station, were planned and executed under the direction of
Messrs. Daukes and Hamilton, architects of the Company.

The Gloucester and Birmingham Railway is $52\frac{1}{2}$ miles
long from terminus to terminus —*viz.* from Gloucester to
Cheltenham $7\frac{1}{4}$ miles, and from Cheltenham to Birmingham $45\frac{1}{4}$. The whole was constructed under the superintendence of Capt. W. S. Moorson, the Company's engineer.
The original capital of the Company was £950,000, but the
cost of the undertaking amounted to nearly a million and a

half sterling, the difference being raised by an issue of quarter shares, by mortgage debentures, and by loan notes, for which interest at 5 per cent. has to be paid. The portion of the line between Cheltenham and Gloucester is intended to be used in common by the Cheltenham and Great Western Union and the Gloucester and Birmingham Companies, whenever the former shall have completed its line, and so be enabled to avail itself of the full advantages of its act of incorporation.

The trains pass and repass the Cheltenham Station five or six times every day; and omnibusses run from the principal hotels in the town, to meet them, conveying passengers to or fro for a charge of sixpence each.

THE GAS WORKS

are situated at the lower end of the town, on the left of the Tewkesbury road. They are the property of a joint-stock company, established in 1818-19, and incorporated by act of parliament the same year. The great purity of the gas manufactured here is universally admitted, a circumstance which has caused it to be very generally introduced into private houses, as well as into shops and public rooms of every description. Under the able and scientific management of their present superintendent, the Cheltenham gas-works have proved a very lucrative commercial speculation, yielding to the proprietors a handsome interest for the capital embarked, at the same time that the rate of charge to the public for lighting, is less in proportion than in most other towns in the kingdom. The sum required for establishing the company, was £15,000, which was raised in £50 shares, though permission was granted by the act of incorporation to raise a further sum of £10,000, had such a measure been necessary; which, however, it was not. The shares are now at a considerable premium. Mr. T. Spinney is the present manager and superintendent, and resides upon the premises.

WATER WORKS.

As Cheltenham extended its frontier lines of streets, crescents, and terraces, the difficulty of procuring a sufficient supply of pure water was soon felt to be a serious evil. Springs, it is true, were to be met with in almost every situation, but it proved not quite so easy to obtain this element unimpregnated with some mineral, or other foreign matter, which frequently disqualified it for many domestic and culinary purposes. In order, therefore, to remedy this great inconvenience, an Act of Parliament was obtained in 1824, for establishing a public company for the more effectually supplying the town with water from the surrounding hills. Operations were immediately commenced upon a very extensive scale, and the numerous streams and rivulets which rise in the Cotteswold range of hills, were collected into a large reservoir erected for this purpose on the Hewlett Road, about a mile and a half from the High Street. From this reservoir the water was, as it still is, distributed all over the town. It is found to be of the purest description, scarcely showing, when subjected to the most delicate chemical tests, any traces of mineral impregnation. From the great height at which its source is situated, it may be conveyed to the highest stories of all the houses in Cheltenham, without the assistance of any hydraulic apparatus. The capital of the company was £17,500, raised in shares of £250 each. The Act of Parliament had, however, empowered them to increase this by other shares and mortgages to the amount of £13,750 more; but, the original sum proving sufficient, this additional subscription was never required. The shares are now at a considerable premium. The office of the Cheltenham Water Works is at No. 62, Regent Street.

THE CHELTENHAM SEWERS' COMPANY.

This company was incorporated by Act of Parliament in April, 1833, and possesses a capital of £7,500, raised in hundred pound shares. By this Act the company is invested with full powers to make and keep in repair the common sewers and drains of the town; charging those houses who take advantage thereof with an annual rate of payment for their use, yet not compelling any person to use them who, being already in possession of other drains, may not chuse to do so. A main sewer, extending the whole length of the High Street down to the brook at lower Alstone mill, has been completed, and cannot but prove a great benefit and convenience to the inhabitants along that line. A well arranged system of common drainage is of such importance to the general health and cleanliness of every town, that its original projectors and subsequent promoters are alike entitled to the best thanks of the community.

SAVINGS' BANK.

The Cheltenham Provident Institution, or Savings' Bank, was opened November 1st, 1818, and may be truly said to have fully answered the expectations of those benevolent gentlemen who, upon that occasion, came forward as its patrons and supporters, and who have ever since devoted considerable time and attention to its interests, from a conviction that much good could not but result to the poor, from their being induced to cultivate habits of prudence and economy in the appropriation of the little funds which Providence may have placed at their disposal. The Cheltenham Savings' Bank is conducted upon the same plan, and is subjected to the same regulations, as by act of Parliament are binding upon all similar establishments throughout the kingdom; and these being now so generally and perfectly understood, we are spared the necessity of here entering further into detail with the subject. The Bank Office is situated at No. 94, High Street, and is open for receiving deposits, and transacting any other business connected therewith, every Thursday, from twelve o'clock till two. Mr. R. Masters, who resides upon the premises, is the present actuary and secretary.

BANKS.

There are in Cheltenham four Joint Stock Banks, all of which are of some years standing, and bear a high character. They consist of—

The County of Gloucester Bank (late Pitt, Gardner, and Co.'s), 106, High Street; Capital, 8000 Shares at £100; W. Pitt and J. H. Bowly, Managers.—London Agents, Robarts, Curtis, and Co.

Gloucestershire Banking Company, (late Hartland and Co.'s), 394, High Street; Capital, 10,000 Shares at £50; F. Addams, Manager.—London Agents, Williams, Deacon, and Co.

Cheltenham and Gloucestershire Bank, Clarence Street; Capital, 10,000 Shares at £50; W. Ridler, Manager.—London Agents, the London and Westminster Banks.

Branch National Provincial Bank of England, 398, High Street; Capital, 10,000 Shares at £100; J. Cox, Manager.— London Agents, London Joint Stock Bank.

CHAPTER XI.

LOCAL GOVERNMENT AND ADMINISTRATION.

Magistrates—Parochial Authorities—Police Establishment—Town Commissioners—Paving and Lighting—Public Conveyances—Cheltenham Union Poor House.

So much of the prosperity of every place depends upon its government, that we shall scarcely fulfil our duty, as the Stranger's Guide through Cheltenham, unless we direct his attention to the constitution of those authorities in whom are vested the powers of legal direction and controul in respect to all matters affecting its internal economy, and the local administration of justice. In default of chartered and corporate functionaries, the management of all affairs of a public character relating to the town devolve, in Cheltenham, upon the Magistrates, the Board of Commissioners, and the usual parochial officers; each body having its own peculiar department of responsibilities.

THE MAGISTRATES

meet, in petty sessions, at the Public Office, High Street, every Monday, Thursday, and Saturday, for the purpose of transacting the parochial and police business of the town and neighbourhood, enforcing the provisions of the local acts of Parliament, and directing all other matters connected with the due administration of justice. Besides the days above named, the attendance of Magistrates may be obtained at any time when cases of emergency require their presence for the "despatch of business." G. E. Williams, Esq., clerk to the Magistrates, will be found at all times ready to afford strangers every necessary information as to the duties of the Public Office.

Cheltenham being a non-corporate town, the Magistrates are all competent to act for the county, being appointed in the customary way by the Lord-Lieutenant— an office, at present, filled by Earl Fitzhardinge, upon whom that dignity was conferred Dec. 8, 1835, on the death of the Duke of Beaufort, his lordship's immediate predecessor. Most of the Magistrates are Commissioners of Assessed Taxes, and seven of those acting for the Cheltenham district have been constituted " Commissioners for the General Purposes" of the Income Tax Act, and five others as " Additional Commissioners," upon which honorary bodies, assisted, of course, by the usual stipendiary officers, devolve the responsible duties of carrying into effect the provisions of the law in queston, so far as the borough and parish of Cheltenham are concerned.

A list of the Magistrates acting for the Cheltenham division of the county, is published regularly in " *The Cheltenham Annuaire and Directory.*"

THE PAROCHIAL AUTHORITIES,

considered strictly such, consist of two Churchwardens and four Overseers, who are elected annually by " the parish in vestry assembled," and upon whom devolve the responsibility of managing an important class of the public affairs, particularly the levying and collection of the various local rates and assessments, and the performance of numerous other duties attaching to their respective offices. There are likewise certain paid collectors, constables, &c., who hold their appointments under the above functionaries, or under the Board of Guardians. And, in addition to all these, there are certain MANORIAL OFFICERS, as the High Bailiff, Steward of the Manor, Constables, Tything-men, &c., who, however, have for the most part a mere nominal authority—acting, as they do, under the Lord of the Manor, who, by his Steward, holds a Court Leet twice in every year; at one of which these feudal functionaries are annually appointed. The Manor Office is in Portland Street.

THE POLICE ESTABLISHMENT

of Cheltenham was formerly subject to the authority and controul of the Commissioners for the town, who maintained a body of day and night constables for the public protection, and the preservation of order and decorum. But on the establishment of the county constabulary force, in 1840, and the appointment of Cheltenham as the head-quarters of the district, with a full complement of police officers—the force formerly kept up by the Commissioners was withdrawn and disbanded, and the security of life and property, and the peace and quiet of the place, confided to their newly organized successors, who have certainly acquitted themselves well in the discharge of their onerous and unpopular duties. The residence of the chief constable is in Cheltenham. The barracks or station of the police force is in St. George's Place, where one or more of the superintendents is constantly in attendance. The expense of maintaining this new police establishment is defrayed out of the county fund—the quota of Cheltenham, as of all other places in the shire, being levied on the poor rates.

———

THE PUBLIC COMMISSIONERS

hold their meetings at the Fleece Inn, the first Friday, in every month, for the purpose of taking cognizance of all matters connected with the local government of the place, plenary powers being vested in them for this purpose by an act of parliament passed in the year 1821 (2nd Geo. IV.); by which act they are also empowered to frame such bye-laws and rules as to them shall appear necessary for the peace, security, and general interests of the town. The paving and lighting the streets and highways, and the regulation and superintendence of the flys and public conveyances, are, therefore, comprehended within their peculiar province. They also possess the power of levying rates, in order to carry the several provisions of their act into full effect.

PAVING AND LIGHTING.—The state of our public streets and thoroughfares bears ample testimony to the benefits resulting from the superintendence of the Board of Commissioners. Perhaps in no other town in the kingdom is such order and neatness observed. Every possible attention is paid to its cleanliness, by prohibiting, or where this is impracticable by immediately removing, every nuisance and obstruction whatsoever from the highways and bye-ways. In summer all the principal streets are regularly watered, and in winter as regularly cleansed, by public scavengers. The pavements are generally broad, and securely laid down; while in the lighting department, the High Street of Cheltenham may fairly challenge any town in the kingdom to surpass it for brilliancy, there being in it alone upwards of one hundred public lamps, and distributed through the different parts of the town, between five and six hundred more; the gas itself being of a very superior quality. These lamps are always lighted at or within half an hour after sunset, and continue burning in May, June, and July, until three o'clock a.m.; in August, September, March, and April, till four o'clock, and in October, November, December, January, and February, till six o'clock. All the main streets are provided with capacious sewers, for carrying off the waste water and common drainage of every description, so that no nuisance is suffered to accumulate. Every care, in short, is taken by the Commissioners to ensure the general health of the town; and for their ever-successful exertions in this particular they are entitled to the highest praise.

THE PUBLIC CONVEYANCES mostly in use in Cheltenham, are small one-horse carriages, called *Flys*, and Wheel Chairs; and the regulation of these forms one of the especial duties of the Town Commissioners, by whom they require to be licensed from year to year. A number of stands are appointed in different parts of the town, where and where only, these vehicles are authorized to ply for public hire. The charges which they are entitled to make, are regulated according to the distance gone over, or the time occupied, as may be agreed; and also, so far as regards the Flys, according to the number of persons conveyed—herein differing from the Hackney Coach regulations of the metropolis and other places. For the guidance of strangers, we annex the Table of Fares authorized by the Commissioners.

TABLE OF FARES FOR CHAIRS AND CARRIAGES.

FARES FOR DISTANCE.	Sedan Chairs.	Fly Carriages Drawn by Men.		Wheel Chairs.	Fly and other Carriages, drawn by one Horse.			Fly and other Carriages, more than one Horse.
		One Person.	Two Persons.		One Person.	Two Persons.	Three Persons or more.	One or more.
Not exceeding a ¼ of a mile, or 440 yards ..	0 6	0 6	0 9	0 6	....	....	....	....
Every ¼ of a mile commenced beyond the 1st ¼	0 6	0 6	0 9	....	....	....	....	....
Beyond a ¼ of a mile, and not exceeding ½ mile	....	....	....	0 9	....	....	....	....
Beyond ½ a mile, and not exceeding ¾	....	....	....	1 0	....	....	....	....
Beyond ¾ and not exceeding one mile	....	....	....	1 6	....	....	....	....
Any distance not exceeding one mile	....	....	....	....	0 9	1 0	1 6	1 6
Beyond 1 mile, and not exceeding 1½ mile ..	....	....	....	2 0	1 3	1 6	2 0	2 3
Beyond 1½ mile, and not exceeding 2 miles ..	....	....	....	2 6	2 0	2 0	2 6	3 6
Every other half mile commenced	....	....	....	....	0 6	0 6	0 6	0 6

FARES FOR TIME—*Within the Distance of Four Miles from the Centre Stone of Cheltenham.*

	Sedan Chairs.	Fly Carriages Drawn by Men.		Wheel Chairs.	Fly and other Carriages, drawn by one Horse.			Fly and other Carriages, more than one Horse.
		One Person.	Two Persons.		One Person.	Two Persons.	Three Persons or more.	One or more.
Not exceeding one hour	2 6	2 6	3 0	1 6	2 6	2 6	2 6	4 0
Every other ½ hour commenced beyond 1 hour	1 3	1 3	1 6	0 9	1 0	1 0	1 0	1 6

** After One o'clock in the Morning, the Fares shall be increased one half more than the above Sums, until Six o'clock in the Morning.

Two Children under Ten Years of age, to be considered as ONE Passenger.

UNION POOR HOUSE.

Cheltenham forms the centre of a district, comprising, in addition to its own parish, those of Badgworth, Charlton Kings, Cowley, Cubberley, Leckhampton, Prestbury, Shurdington, Staverton, Swindon-up-Hatherley, Great Witcombe, and the hamlet of Uckington, which are formed under the provisions of the New Poor Law, into one Union —for the reception of whose poor a large and commodious building has lately been erected in the Swindon road; the former parish workhouse, near St. James's Square, having been converted into schools for the instruction and employment of the pauper children. The management of the Union, and all affairs connected therewith, is undertaken by the Board of Guardians, who meet every Thursday, at the poor house, for that purpose.

The cost of erecting the new Union Poor House, which amounted, with the purchase of the land, to about £8000, is now in course of being defrayed by instalments, out of the poor rates—the parish having raised the sum necessary for its erection by loans on interest, which are to be liquidated by annual payments, extending over a period of twenty years from the date of their contraction.

The Union Poor House is open for the inspection of visitors every Monday afternoon, from two to five o'clock.

CHAPTER XII.

PRINCIPAL STREETS.

*High Street—The Promenade—Promenade Villas—Bays Hill Estate—
Montpellier—Suffolk Square and Lawn—Park Place—Lansdown
Place, Crescent, and Terrace—Tivoli—Park Estate—Bath Road—
Cambray—Pittville Estate—Clarence and Wellington Squares, &c.*

Having, in the first and second chapters of the present
Work, reviewed the past condition of Cheltenham, and
glanced at its historic existence during the centuries which
followed its first introduction to notice in Doomsday Book;
and also, in the subsequent chapters, described in detail
those various public buildings and establishments which,
one after another, arose into being as the place increased
in size and importance, it now only remains for us to describe the principal streets and thoroughfares of which the
town is composed; or, at least, such of them as are in any
way deserving the notice, or are likely to arrest the attention of the passing stranger.

First, then, of the HIGH STREET, which, dividing the
town into two nearly equal portions, may be said to commence at the Charlton Turnpike, and extend to the Railway bridge on the Tewkesbury road—the distance between
these points being upwards of a mile and a half. The
houses throughout are numbered to nearly five hundred
and were those, which have been built of late years at

N

either extremity, and for the most part separately named,
to be included in the general enumeration, it would be
found that two or three hundred more would have to be
added. A century back the whole of Cheltenham was
comprehended within a very small portion of this noble
street, the length of which, as above given, is scarcely exceeded by that of any other street in the kingdom. Of
the original town, however, there is, probably, not a single
house remaining, and not more than half-a-dozen dating
their foundation a hundred years ago—the thatched roofs
and gable fronts of a former epoch having given place to
the loftier and more elegant structures of modern times.
Two delapidated tenements, opposite Cambray; the architectural antiquity, at the eastern corner of Winchcomb
Street; and the *Schola Grammatica*, below the Market
Arcade—being almost the only remains now existing of
what Cheltenham was, even during its " transition state."

As you enter the High Street, from the London or
Charlton road, the numerous detached villas and rows of
well-built residences, on both sides of the way, form an approach well calculated to produce in the mind of the
stranger a favourable impression of the wealth and beautiful arrangements of the town—an impression which will
be still heightened as he descends towards St. George's
Square—passing on the right an unbroken series of excellent shops and private dwelling houses; among which the
broad fronts of the Belle Vue, the Royal, and the George
Hotels, stand prominently out;—the projecting portico of
the last-named hostelry, and the plate-glass window of
the County of Gloucester Bank, being among the most
recent improvements. On the opposite side of the way,
the Assembly and Club Rooms, with their long line of
iron balcony; and the neatly uniform frontage of the

Plough Hotel, occupying a range of buildings, which, for extent, is unequalled by any other establishment in this leading thoroughfare, are sure to arrest attention. The shops also in this part of the High Street are amongst the best in the town, many of them having handsome and expensive fronts, with windows of plate-glass for the display of the merchandise on sale within. The broad pavement, extending between Cambray and the Colonnade, was formerly the grand lounge of the gay and fashionable visitors of Cheltenham; but since the plantations, forming the walks and drives of the different Spas, have grown up, so as to afford the shelter and cool retreat, which they now do, these have obtained a manifest preference. The best point for obtaining a view of the High Street is from the Royal Hotel, looking down its entire length in the direction of the Public Office.

Next in importance to the busy scene just passed through, and much its superior in interest to the stranger, is THE PROMENADE, which, though entering out of the High Street by the narrow and inconvenient approach of the Colonnade, presents such a novel and characteristic appearance as no other town in the kingdom can exhibit in the arrangement of its public highways. Originally laid out as the grand drive to the Sherborne Spa,* it now forms the most attractive and convenient of all the public thoroughfares: an unbroken line of chesnut, beech, and other deciduous trees extends on either side the carriage road through its entire length; the luxuriant branches overhanging the paved footpaths, constitute vistas of the most picturesque and pleasing description—forming, when the summer foliage is fully developed, covered walks impervious alike to sunshine and the passing shower, and

* See before, p. 17.

inviting at all times to agreeable exercise. That on the
right hand is an especial favourite, and on a fine afternoon is usually thronged with the gayest and most fashionable of the residents and visitors of Cheltenham.
Set back some distance off this " grand parade," is a row
of uniform and well built houses, having projecting balconies to the drawing-room windows. In the centre stands
The Imperial, an Hotel and Boarding House, much frequented at all times, and particularly during the summer
season—its situation being one of the most eligible, as its
internal arrangements are the most perfect and complete
of all the fashionable hostelries of the place. Beyond
this row, and retreating farther from the main road, is a
second series of buildings, formerly distinguished as the
Lower Promenade, but now numbered in continuation of
the first. Built somewhat after the fashion of the Louvre
this range presents a striking and architectural façade—
the long line of arched balconies and iron railings being
judiciously broken by the projection of the centre houses,
forward from the main line, and the introduction to these
of a pillared and pedimented front. A broad carriage
road and a lawn and plantation of ornamental shrubs,
separates this division of the Promenade from the great
stream of thoroughfare constantly flowing between the
High Street and the Montpellier and Lansdown quarters,
situated farther south.

The houses on the eastern side of the Sherborne drive
are called PROMENADE VILLAS. They are less uniform
in architectural appearance than the buildings last described, and are of a more mixed character in the purposes to which they are appropriated—private residences
and public shops alternating each other throughout the
greater portion; the former becoming, every year, fewer

in number, from their conversion to the purposes of trade, which is rapidly extending itself southward of the High Street, necessarily following the stream of traffic, which, since the opening of the Railway Stations, has flowed in this direction with increased and still increasing energy. The most conspicuous building in the line of the Promenade Villas is the Literary and Philosophical Institution, the fine Grecian portico of which cannot fail to arrest the attention of even the most indifferent passer by. The

PROMENADE VILLAS.

view along the pavement in front, and beneath the overarching trees, above which, in the distance, rises the pediment of the Queen's Hotel, is peculiarly animated, and the scene altogether such an one as can be met with only in Cheltenham, and in Cheltenham only on a fine summer's day; or the meteorologic conditions of the atmosphere have a marvellous effect upon the spirit and appearance of this as of every scene, in the changeable climate of England.

At the end of the Promenade Villas, a broad opening on the opposite side of the way, between the *Lower Promenade*, already described, and *Promenade Terrace*, displays the entrance to the BAYS HILL ESTATE, a large tract of land contiguous to the Royal Old Wells, and, until lately, occupied as pasture and orchard grounds, but now traversed by roads and mapped out for extensive building speculation. Already two very handsome rows of houses, called the ROYAL WELL and BAYS HILL TERRACES, have been erected, as also a number of detached villas, many of them displaying considerable taste individally, but collectively forming a strange mixture of the classical, the Italian, the Gothic, and the modern domestic styles of architecture. Several of these villas are occupied by resident families of affluence and station, and others are in an unfinished-state.

Advancing in the direction of the view described, we arrive at the extremity of the Promenade road, where stands the Queen's Hotel, one of the largest and handsomest establishments of its kind in England; and having its internal appointments on a scale of magnificence corresponding to its external appearance. It was erected in 1837-8, on the scite of the former Imperial Pump Room, after plans and designs by R. W. Jearrad, Esq., the architect of Christ Church and other public edifices in the town; and is the property of a Joint Stock Company. It was first opened, for the reception of visitors, on the 21st of July, 1838. From the front of this building the view down the entire extent of the road is peculiarly beautiful, the distant termination being closed in by the white houses of the Colonnade and the High Street, which are seen rising considerably above the trees, and are backed, in the far distance, by Cleeve Cloud, the loftiest of the

THE PROMENADE DRIVE.

Cotteswold range of hills. The dip or descent from the foreground to the middle distance, where an opening in the plantation admits a broad mass of light, and its gentle rise again from this point to that where the vista narrows to its entrance, has a highly pleasing effect, resembling as it does the curve in a long cord stretched to its utmost;—on either side are the footpaths already described, overarched by the green branches of the chesnut and beech, and flanked by the Imperial nursery grounds on the right, and Cambridge Villas and Promenade Terrace on the left.

Eastward of the noble drive just described is IMPERIAL SQUARE, two sides of which are enclosed by excellent houses, set back some distance from the carriage road, and having a double row of trees—remains of the walks and promenades of the Sherborne Spa,—between them and the public highway; the third being shut in by buildings connected with the Queen's Hotel; and the fourth, or western

side, having Cambridge Villas and Promenade Terrace for
its extreme boundary.   In the centre are the gardens and
shrubberies of the Nursery above mentioned, covering an
area of four acres, and forming a beautiful open space overlooked by all the surrounding buildings.

Passing the end of the Queen's Hotel, the principal
thoroughfare here proceeds up a short ascent in front of
a number of excellent shops, towards the Montpellier property, through which it continues to the Lansdown gate,
having the drives and gardens of the Spa on the left, and
the Pump Room and a small oval building, called *The
Museum*, on the right hand.   The claim of the latter to

notice arises from the circumstance of its having been
built by the celebrated mineralogist, Mr. J. Mawe, con-
temporary with the second Pump Room, erected by Mr.
H. Thompson, in the year 1816-17.   It is now used as a
repository for the sale of curiosities and fancy goods.

Among the places called into existence by the attractive influences of the Montpellier establishment, and still

included within the limits of its private drives, are Montpellier Spa Buildings and Montpellier Parade
and Terrace, consisting of neat and convenient houses,
though, for the most part, of unequal size and ununiform
in external appearance: their proximity to the Spas and
their consequently gay and cheerful situations, however,
render them valuable as property, being rarely unoccupied.
The roads and walks in front of these different ranges of
buildings, and of *Vittoria Walk*, which branches off from
the eastern end of Montpellier Parade to Oriel Terrace,
though publicly lighted, are the private property of
P. Thompson, Esq., the owner of the adjacent Spa—an
annual charge of one guinea per annum being levied on
each of the houses towards defraying the expense of keeping them in repair.

An opening, near the top of Montpellier Terrace, leads
into Suffolk Square, which, though still in an incomplete state, contains some of the largest and best houses
in the town: those forming two sides of the Square being
detached, and having large pleasure gardens round them.
The first of these, a low old-fashioned mansion, standing at the north-west corner, was once the residence of
Lord Suffolk, and fifty years ago was the only habitation in existence, in this direction, south of the Chelt.*
Immediately facing Suffolk House, is St. James's Church,
of which an account has already been given. The centre of the Square is laid out as nursery and pleasure
grounds, for the accommodation of the owners and occu-
piers of the surrounding houses. An outlet south opens
immediately opposite Park Place, one of the prettiest
streets in Cheltenham, consisting, for the most part, of re-

---

* Previous to its purchase by Lord Suffolk, it was a mere farm house,
known by the name of " Gallipot Farm."—*Cheltenham Annuaire*, 1838, p. 110.

O

markably neat villas, having small lawns and gardens in front, which, being planted with flowering and other ornamental shrubs, have, especially in the summer season, a peculiarly cheerful appearance.

We will not, however, at present proceed farther in this direction, but turning round to the right continue along the footpath which leads to SUFFOLK LAWN, a series of

Suffolk Lawn.

noble looking mansions, backing the western side of the Square we have just left, and having before them a row of lofty and magnificent elms, bounded by the new Painswick road, which winds along here to its junction with the Bath road branch, about a mile on the Shurdington road. The view of Suffolk Lawn, as seen in profile, from the end near the Montpellier gate, and through the vista formed by the stately trees above alluded to, and the porticoed fronts of the houses, is the finest of its kind in Cheltenham, resembling rather some of the palace scenes of Italy, than the suburb of an English borough.

At angles with Suffolk Lawn, and running out due west from the entrance to the Montpellier drives, is the new Gloucester road, having LANSDOWN PLACE on its right hand. This handsome row was commenced in 1825, by P. Thompson, Esq., and subsequently continued by R. W. Jearrad, Esq., from whose architectural designs were built those houses forming the upper division of the series, which are of a much superior description to those erected on the original plan, being more lofty and substantial in appearance, and having elegant balconies partly open and partly converted into conservatories, running along their fronts. The entire range forms altogether one of the most fashionable " quarters " of the town, as indeed it well deserves to be, from the character and quality of the buildings, as well as from the highly favourable situation in which they are placed, having an aspect due south. Green lawns and pleasure grounds, stocked with ornamental shrubs, and enclosed by iron railings, extend along the whole line, separating the public from the private highway, with a pavement of unusual width, forming a favourite promenade, which, during the summer season, is generally thronged with company. At the very end of this stands the *Lansdown Hotel and Boarding House*, the most recently established of the public hostelries of the place; and, from its cheerful situation, not unlikely soon to become a favourite one.

On the road-side, nearly opposite, are two remarkably fine sycamores, which the curious naturalist will find deserving an " attentive perusal," nor can they well escape the notice of the lover of the picturesque, forming, as they do, conspicuous objects in the view, from either extremity

of the Lansdown road.   Some yards behind this " noble
pair " is a group of American poplars, consisting also of

American Poplars.

two trees, that seem to tell of the " forest days " of a by-
gone generation, exhibiting a great deal of wild-wood
beauty and character in the development of their spreading
branches.   From the windows of HATHERLEY PLACE,—a
row of excellent houses, which, commencing at this point,
runs southward towards *The Park*,—these poplars, when in
full foliage, are seen to great advantage, forming as they do
the principal foreground object in a landscape of large extent and much beauty; and which, from the Lansdown
Hotel, seen rising above the trees on the right, stretches
out far northward to the Malvern Hills, at the base of
which, on a clear day, may be distinctly seen the white
houses of that pleasant town.

Here, where the old tramway crosses the Lansdown
road, the latter separates into two branches—one diverging
to the right, and called the *Queen's Road*, leading to the

railway stations—the other holding its original turnpike course as the King's highway to Gloucester. A number of detached private residences of the best class have been, within late years, built along the northern line of this road; but we must leave these suburban objects, and, turning up to the right, proceed to examine the more important and densely disposed buildings on the LANSDOWN ESTATE.

Passing up the opening, immediately opposite the two large Sycamore trees above-mentioned, and between the new hotel and a low dilapidated building, called Westhall, one of the oldest houses in this part of Cheltenham,—and, from its present uninhabited state, evidently intended to be shortly removed altogether—we have before us a pretty view up the road in front of LANSDOWN PARADE, a series of small but genteel residences; and a number of detached villas rising one above the other as the ground ascends towards Christ Church, the majestic tower of which forms a striking and beautiful object in the distance beyond and above the whole.

To the right of the Parade is LANSDOWN CRESCENT, consisting of forty-nine lofty and excellent houses, having an uniform elevation throughout, and peculiarly adapted, from their internal arrangements, for the accommodation of families of the first respectability. The chord-line of this Crescent measures 1510 feet, and the curve is, consequently, of very considerable extent, having the horns facing east and north-west. The houses along the latter division command extensive views in the direction of the Malvern hills; those forming the eastern segment of the curve looking over the Bays Hill estate in a townward direction.

Opposite a break in the Crescent, and at the corner of the road proceeding thence to Christ Church, along the front of Lansdown Terrace, are two elegant VILLAS, built in the Italian style, after designs by Mr. R. W. Jearrad, by whom indeed the whole of the Lansdown estate was planned, and under whose personal superintendance nearly all the houses at present in being there have been erected;—in ornamental appearance they are unquestionably the most attractive of all the detached houses in Cheltenham, and occupy situations most unexceptionable, retiring some distance from the road, with gardens before them, and having a due south aspect.

LANSDOWN TERRACE, built along the ground ascending towards Christ Church, and set back some distance from the public road, forms an imposing row of buildings, having elevations three stories in height, and of a highly architectural appearance—the basements being protected by a continuous line of stone balustrades, and the drawing-room fronts having stone balconies with pillars supporting well proportioned pediments, uniform in character, extending throughout the range, which facing due west, commands a beautiful landscape view over the vale country, in the direction of Gloucester, having the church-crowned Chosen, rising picturesquely in the middle distance.

There are a number of very superior detached mansions on the western slope and on the brow of the hill facing the upper end of Lansdown Terrace, among the most curious of which are *Abancourt*, two gothic looking villas built in the Tudor style of domestic architecture, and *Tyrol Villa*, an exceedingly neat adaptation of Swiss designs.

The land contiguous to and beyond the Lansdown estate has been mapped out to a very large extent for building purposes, and will, doubtless, in a few years, become an important suburb to the town, filling up the vacant space between it and the Railway station, situated

at its western limit. Hitherto, however, Christ Church is the only building which has been erected on the property. It is not necessary, therefore, that we should proceed farther in this direction at present.

Returning now from the fashionable quarter of Lansdown, we proceed along Suffolk Lawn, to inspect a part of the town scarcely, indeed, yet included within its limits, having only of late years become united to it by the extension and opening of new lines of communication. Among the best of these is TIVOLI, a street running parallel with *Park Place,* and, like it, consisting almost wholly of detached villas, with small gardens or lawns in front, enclosed within iron railings. Several of these villas display considerable taste in their arrangement, particularly one called *St. Oswald's,* on the right hand side of the way, affording, on a small scale, an excellent example of the application of gothic designs to modern buildings.

The upper end of *Tivoli,* opens into THE PARK, an estate comprising upwards of one hundred acres, and which, ten or twelve years ago, was laid out with great taste and judgment by T. Billings, Esq., the then proprietor of the land. The main feature of Mr. Billings' plan consists in a circular or rather oval carriage drive, nearly a mile in circuit and seventy feet in width, having, on either side, broad gravelled footpaths, planted with ornamental trees and shrubs, forming a continuous screen, and the larger branches of which overarching the walks above, give to the greenwood vistas thus produced, an effect peculiarly scenic —the varieties of the foliage, the changing hues of light and shade, and the occasional breaks in the enclosures, through which snatches of bright landscape become ever and anon exposed, render these walks among the most delightful in Cheltenham, particularly during the summer.

On passing from Tivoli, and turning to the right into
the estate here spoken of, one of the first objects that arrests attention is the entrance and Lodge of the PARK
GARDENS, designed, with great taste, by S. W. Daukes,
Esq., the present owner of the grounds within.*   These

The Lodge of the Park Gardens.

Gardens, with their enclosures and surrounding Plantations, cover an area of twenty acres, forming the centre of
the drive along which we are proceeding, and preserving
for the houses built and building round its outer circle, a
free and beautiful look out.   These are all of a very superior description, and many of them mansions of large extent and imposing appearance, though observing no uniformity of architectural design or arrangement—fancy and
the tastes of their respective owners having dictated the
style and plan of each.   There is, however, one elegant

* Of these, as public Gardens and Pleasure Grounds, an account has been
already given.— See before, p. 97.

little villa on this estate, which deserves more particular notice: it is called *Tudor Lodge*, and stands at the corner

Tudor Lodge.

of a private road opening out of the eastern side of the drive, not far from the Park Place entrance. So happy, and withal so faithful an adaptation of the principles and peculiarities of gothic architecture to modern mansions, is rarely to be met with, doing infinite credit to the taste, skill, and professional knowledge of its talented architect, W. S. Daukes, Esq., who, in working out this unique little model, has obviously been as carefully attentive to the historical accuracy of the details of his design as to the general plan—the decorations and finishings of every part exhibiting throughout the most perfect harmony.

At the Park Place entrance into the estate which we have just walked round, are several excellent detached residences, and a peculiarly neat Lodge—this approach having been originally designed as the principal one into the property, the oval drive above described meeting here at its point of divergence.

The return walk townward may be varied by turning down the road at right angles with Park Place, and which, crossing the Painswick or new Bath road, passes, on the left, the little church of St. Phillips, which we have already

P

noticed, and opens a short distance above into the Leck-hampton and Birdlip road, where several buildings of peculiar interest invite attention; of these the noblest in external appearance, as well as the richest in internal attractions, is *Thirlestane House*, the residence of Lord Northwick, of whose Picture Gallery and Paintings we

Thirlestane House and Picture Gallery.

have already given a brief notice.* Being surrounded by a high stone wall the house is not well seen from the public road, though its finely classic front rises sufficiently conspicuous above the interposing barrier, to call forth the admiration, and excite the curiosity of all, who, passing from Cheltenham along the Bath road, obtain, in doing so, the best view of the building which its situation admits of, from without.

From the corner of Suffolk road, which opens imme-

* See before p. 110.

diately opposite the north-western angle of Thirlestane House, an excellent view may be had of the new PRO-PRIETARY COLLEGE—one of the most ornamental as it assuredly is one of the most important buildings in the town. The institution, for whose use it has been erected, was established in 1841, for the instruction of the sons of the resident gentry, who here receive an education of the most liberal and comprehensive character, at an exceedingly moderate cost—the nomination of a shareholder being required to secure a scholar admission. The management of the establishment is vested in a Board of Directors, who have the entire controul of its affairs—the appointment of the masters for the various departments, and the general superintendance of the affairs of the proprietary, whom they represent. The beautiful and characteristic pile of building which we are now contemplating, was erected from designs by J. Wilson, Esq., an architect of much celebrity in this part of the kingdom, and whose professional reputation has certainly not been impaired by this additional evidence of skill and ability. It is built in the perpendicular English style of the 16th century, having a large and handsome bay window at its west end, lighting the principal school-room. The funds raised for the structure by the proprietors, not having been sufficiently ample to perfect the design in all its details, some of the more ornamental portions, as the series of crocketted pinnacles, rising from the battlemented parapet, have been, for the present, omitted, thus maring, in a degree, the general effect intended by the architect. The college was first opened in June, 1843, when the annual prizes to the scholars for proficiency in their respective studies, and for moral conduct, were publicly awarded in the large class room.

Descending the Bath road, between the College on the right, and *Sandford Place* on the left hand, we pass in succession two or three rows of excellent private dwelling houses, among which are *Paragon Parade* and *Buildings, Bath Buildings*, and *Oriel Place*, opposite to which is the National School, and, at the end, a wide opening, called *Oriel Terrace*, communicating with the Montpellier drives and Imperial Square.   Proceeding still onward we pass on the same side of the way the long low buildings of the Montpellier Baths and Cheltenham Salts' Laboratory, and a few paces beyond obtain a glimpse of the waters of the Chelt!—*i.e.* when there are any waters in its course!—at the only place, during its progress through the town, where this stream is now open to sunlight and the breeze. Turning to the left into *Bath Street* we now find ourselves in *Cambray*, which enters the High Street a short distance above the Assembly Rooms.

Having passed through some of the principal thorough-fares of the southern districts of the town, we may now pay a hasty visit to a few of the places most entitled to notice situated north of the High Street: proceeding, therefore, from the Plough Hotel up *Winchcomb Street*, the direct though narrow and unworthy approach to the Pittville Spa, we pass, some distance up, on the right hand, the *Female Orphan Asylum*, and, at the very top of the street, on the left, *Columbia Place*, a row of private houses much superior in external appearance to those already passed.

Exactly facing the end of Winchcomb Street, a pair of massive and elaborately wrought iron gates mark the en-trance into the PITTVILLE ESTATE, the public road here branching off on the right to Prestbury, and on the left, at an acuter angle, in front of *Pittville Terrace* to Clarence Square. Advancing through the gates in question we enter the private walks and drives conducting to the Spa which has given name and importance to the surrounding property. Immediately within, on the east side, is *Segrave Place*, and on the west, a number of large and substantial villas. Beyond these, and lying between the Evesham road and the principal drive, are the gardens and pleasure grounds of the estate, which are kept in beautiful order for the convenience and recreation of the surrounding inhabitants, having a broad gravelled walk meandering through its lawns, and issuing at the foot of the western bridge which leads to the Pump Room. The largest row upon the property is *Pittville Lawn*, a series of fourteen or fifteen excellent houses, several of them detached and separately named, and differing greatly from each other in size and architectural appearance, and all occupied by families of ample independent fortune. With an aspect nearly west, and overlooking the lawns and pleasure grounds above noticed, the situation of Pittville Lawn may be pronounced, in every respect, most unexceptionable.

The grand drive to the Pittville Spa is intersected by others which pass eastward into the Prestbury road, and westward into that of Cleeve, the latter connecting itself with Portland Street, forms the principal northern outlet of the town, and, for a considerable distance, is flanked on either hand by buildings of the best description, consisting of detached mansions and rows of buildings in different stages of completeness: among the latter *Pittville Parade* stands out most prominently, forming as it does a peculiarly neat and uniform range on the left, and exactly parallel with the road. Behind Pittville Parade is *Clarence*

Square, containing a number of genteel houses, enclosing four sides of an ample area, the centre of which is laid out as pleasure gardens—the roads exterior and in front of the houses being tastefully planted with trees already grown to a considerable height, and affording shade and picturesque beauty to the entire neighbourhood. Beyond, and opening immediately out of Clarence Square, is another similar brick and mortar speculation, called *Wellington Square*, around which several large and handsome houses have been built within the last ten years. Passing hence into the Cleeve road, a short distance above Pittville Parade, we may now proceed onward to the Pittville Spa, or return down Portland and Pittville Streets to the grand centre of our town, terminating our rambles at the best possible of all halting places for strangers—the Plough Hotel.

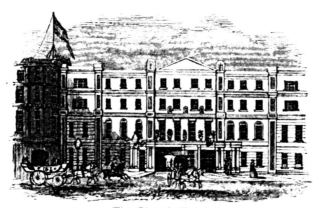

The Plough Hotel.

APPENDIX.—No. I.

CHRONOLOGICAL NOTICES OF CHELTENHAM,

AND

EVENTS CONNECTED WITH ITS HISTORY,

FROM THE EARLIEST RECORDED PERIOD TO THE CLOSE OF 1842.

1011—St. Mary's Church built.

The date here given is that commonly received as the year of the erection of this church, though it cannot be proved with any degree of certainty. A Priory was known to have existed in Cheltenham, which was supposed to have been founded about the year 803.

1081—Cheltenham first noticed in Doomsday Book.

This is the earliest recorded mention of the town, where it appears under the name of *Chintenham,* and is described as consisting of eight hydes and a half of land held by King Edward. On pulling down the old Market House, in 1817, a stone was discovered bearing an inscription of the date of 1107.

1574—Alms Houses founded by Richard Pate, Esq.

Free Grammar School ditto.

Pate's Alms Houses are situated in Albion Street, for the reception of six poor pople, two of whom, by the conditions of the grant, must be women. The Free Grammar School is in High Street, adjoining Yearsley's Hotel. The nomination of the Head Master is vested in Corpus Christi College. That office is at present filled by the Rev. W. H. Hawkins, B.D.

1628—Manor of Cheltenham sold to John Dutton, Esq., of
　　　Sherborne, for £1200.

　　　The first Manorial Court was held, in virtue of this sale, the 3rd of
　　　June, 1629.

1660—Quakers' Meeting House built.

1667—Poor's Ground purchased.

　　　The Poor's Ground here spoken of consists of several plots of
　　　ground, situated near the Shackles Turnpike. They were originally
　　　purchased with monies, bequeathed by various persons, for the
　　　general purposes of charity. The proceeds, amounting to about
　　　£60 per annum, continue to be annually distributed by the Church-
　　　wardens on St. Thomas's Day to poor people upwards of sixty
　　　years of age,—the preference being given to those born in the
　　　parish.

1660—Rev. Maurice Roberts, first incumbent of Cheltenham
　　　after the Restoration.

　　　Of the Curates of Cheltenham previous to the restoration no suf-
　　　ficiently authentic account is in existence. The nomination at this
　　　time was vested in Jesus College.

1666—Population, 1500; Inhabited Houses, 321.

1701—Baptist Chapel built.

1703—Terrible storm, November 27th.

　　　That this was a storm of unusual violence may be inferred from the
　　　fact of its being especially noticed in the Parish Register, where
　　　the following account is given:—" A terrible tempestuous wind on
　　　the 27th day of November, about ye hours from one to seven in
　　　the morning, which did very great damage, Both at Sea and alsoe
　　　in Land, to the ruind of very many ffamilies."

1716—Mineral Spring discovered.

　　　For the particulars of this as well as all subsequent discoveries and
　　　improvements connected with the Spas, vide p.

1718—The well railed in and covered.

1721—Waters first analysed by Drs. Greville and Baird.

1731—June 5, Storm of lightning and hail.

　　　This storm is said to have destroyed property to the amount of
　　　£2000, and as the number of inhabited houses could not have ex-

ceeded 400, nor the population 2000, it may be inferred that it was one of extraordinary severity.

1738—Dome built over the Well.

This dome formerly occupied the centre of the Old Well Walk, between the present Pump Room and the private house. It was removed in the Spring of 1837. It was also in 1738 that the Well was first called *The Cheltenham Spa*.

1739—The avenue of elm trees planted.

1749—Dr. Jenner born at Berkeley, May 17th.

1774—Long Room at the Old Well erected.

Down to this date the house, now a private Dwelling, had been used as the pump room.

1780—Simeon Moreau, Esq., elected first M.C.

In consequence of the influx of Visitors, which, in this year, was estimated at 360, it was deemed expedient to appoint a Master of the Ceremonies, and the above gentleman was accordingly elected to the office.

1781—Falconberg House built.

This house is celebrated from having been the residence of King George the Third. It is now called Bay's Hill Lodge.

1784—James Dutton, Esq., created Lord Sherborne.

1786—Paving Commissioners' Act passed.

This Act (the first passed for the purpose of cleansing and improving the town) was repealed, together with a second Act for amending the same, passed twenty years afterwards, by the present Town Commissioners' Act in the year 1821.

1787—Freeman's Baths established.

These baths are entitled to notice from having been the first public baths opened in Cheltenham.

1787—Sunday Schools established.

1788—July 12, George the Third arrived.

July 21, Prince of Wales arrived.

August 1, Duke of York arrived.

August 16, Royal Family left.

To this visit of the Royal Family Cheltenham is indebted for much of its reputation as the resort of fashion,—the fame which it ac-

quired by thus becoming the temporary sojourn of Royalty having
materially contributed to its present prosperity.

1795—First Troop of Gloucestershire Yeomanry Cavalry, — Snell,
　　　Esq., Commandant.

Three years after the formation of this troop (viz. in 1798), a
Corps of Volunteer Infantry was raised, of which Sir W. Hicks,
Bart., was appointed Captain.

1797—Population 2700; Inhabited Houses 530.

1799—Rev. Henry Foulkes appointed Incumbent.

Mr. Foulkes was the last Curate appointed by Jesus College subject to the original restrictions, which required, among other conditions, that the holder of the Curacy should be a Bachelor and an
M.A. of three years standing.

1801—Population 3076; Inhabited Houses 710.

1801—The Delabere property purchased by Henry Thompson,
　　　Esq., and called the Montpellier.

The property purchased by Mr. H. Thompson consisted of between
three and four hundred acres, extending from beyond Lansdown
into the Bath Road and Sandford Fields. A short time prior to
Mr. Thompson's purchase the Earl of Suffolk had bought about
thirty acres adjoining, with a farm house, (now Suffolk House) for
which he gave the sum of £2,800. His daughter, Lady Catherine
Howard, subsequently disposed of the property for £14,000. Suffolk Lawn and Suffolk Square stand upon a portion of Lord
Suffolk's land.

1801—Simeon Moreau, Esq., M.C., died.

1801—James King, Esq., elected M.C.

1802—Volunteer Infantry disembodied.

1803—Original Chalybeate Spa discovered by Mr. Cruickshanks.

This Spa, which was the first pure chalybeate discovered in Cheltenham, has long since been disused. It was situate in a meadow
behind the present Belle Vue Place. Mr. Cruickshanks was Chemist to the Board of Ordinance.

1805—Theatre built by J. Watson.

Mr. Watson was an itinerant coadjutor of John Kemble and his
sister Mrs. Siddons, who, in the early part of their career, occasionally acted at Cheltenham in a temporary theatre.

1806—Female Orphan Asylum established by Queen Charlotte.

1807—Cambray Chalybeate discovered.

1808—Spring at the Old Well enlarged to 12ft. deep and 6ft. wide.

1809—Montpellier Pump Room opened.

> Previous to the erection of a Pump Room on the scite of the present Rotunda, Mr. Thompson had endeavoured to appropriate Vittoria House (which was built by him and then called Hygæia House) to that purpose, and accordingly had the various spa waters conveyed there through pipes; but, finding the visitors preferred drinking them nearer to their source, he was induced to erect a room immediately over the well, where, ever since, the waters have been drank.

1809—Alstone Spa established.

1809—Cheltenham Chronicle published, price 6d.

> This was the first Newspaper published in Cheltenham, at a time when the population was about 7000.

1809—August 2nd, Cheltenham Chapel opened by the Rev. Rowland Hill and the Rev. W. Jay.

1809—Nov. 21, First stone of the Tram Road from Cheltenham to Gloucester laid by the Earl of Suffolk.

> The ostensible object for forming this Road was the conveying of coal from the Forest of Dean, and hard stone from Bristol for the repair of the roads, the soft stone of Leckhampton having, heretofore, been the only material procurable for that purpose.

1810—Roman Catholic Chapel opened.

1810—June 4, New Assembly Rooms opened with a Ball.

1810—July 2, Leckhampton and Cheltenham Tram Road opened.

> This Tram Road was opened with a public procession, and celebrated by a dinner, at which the Hon. John Dutton, the present Lord Sherborne, presided.

1810—Organ in St. Mary's Church built.

> The expense of this Organ was defrayed by public subscription: it was opened in May 1811.

1811—Population according to census 8325; Inhabited Houses 1556.

1811—June 28th, Decision of the House of Lords on the Berkeley
Peerage question.

By this decision, which refused to recognize the marriage said to
have taken place between the late Earl of Berkeley and the present
Dowager Countess, in the year 1785, Thomas Morton Fitzharding
Berkeley became the acknowledged Earl of Berkeley.

1812—Sept. 22, Foundation stone of Ebenezer Chapel laid.

1813—May 3, Cheltenham Dispensary established.

A Parish Meeting was held in the Vestry on the 3rd of March in
this year, to establish a Dispensary, the Rev. A. Foulkes in the
chair. Drs. Jameson, Parry, Boisragon, and Christie offered themselves as Physicians. On the 9th another meeting was held at the
Assembly Rooms—Lord Ashtown in the chair—at which meeting
a code of regulations and rules was submitted by Dr. Parry, and
adopted. Drs. Jameson and Parry were chosen, by lot, as Physicians, and Messrs. Seager and Newell, Surgeons for the ensuing
year. A Casualty Ward was subsequently added, and in 1836 the
Cheltenham Dispensary was converted into a General Hospital.

1813—September 15, Ebenezer Chapel opened.

1813—September 7th, Mr. Sadler, jun., ascended in his Balloon.

The Balloon had been previously exhibited in the Assembly Rooms
for several weeks, and was to have ascended on the 6th, but was
prevented doing so by the rain. The gas employed for inflating
this Balloon was obtained from sulphuric acid and iron filings, but
although 35cwt. of the former, and a ton and a half of the latter
were consumed, the gas produced was found insufficient to bear
Mr. Sadler's weight; when his son, a youth of 16, took his place,
and effected the ascent. The Balloon descended safely the same
evening at Chipping Norton.

1813—August 2nd, Louis XVIIIth visited Cheltenham.

1813—August 14th, New Bath Road through Cambray opened.

1813—August 9, Sarah Humphries buried in the Cross Road for
felo-de-se.

This was the last instance of a Cross-road Burial in the neighbourhood of Cheltenham.

1816—September 1st, Rev. Charles Jervis appointed Incumbent.

The Rev. Charles Jervis succeeded the Rev. H. Foulkes, and was

the first Curate appointed, subject to the new regulations introduced on the presentation to the curacy being transferred from
Jesus College to the late Joseph Pitt, Esq., who gave in exchange
for it the advowson of Bagenden Church. Mr. Pitt subsequently
sold it to the Trustees in whom the presentation is now vested.
The late Rev. C. Simeon, of Trinity College, Cambridge, was one
of the original Trustees.

1816—June 5, National School established.

A public meeting held on this day at the Assembly Rooms resolved
upon the establishment of a school of this description, and, the re-
solution being promptly supported by patronage and subscription,
was immediately commenced, though the first school room was
not opened until the 6th of January in the following year.

1816— July 7th, Duke of Wellington's first visit.

1816—July 29, Assembly Rooms opened by the Duke of Wellington.

1816—August 9, Mrs. Forty died, aged 72.

Mrs. Hannah Forty was for nearly half a century Pumper at the
Old Well, which was then better known as Mrs. Forty's Well.
Her name is, therefore, intimately associated with the History of
that Spa.

1816—August 9, Countess of Huntingdon's Chapel opened.

1816—October 16, J. King, Esq., M.C., died, aged 70.

1816—Alexander Fothringham, Esq., elected M.C.

1817—January 6, National School opened.

Dr. Bell's system of national education was first publicly recognized
and established in Cheltenham on the 5th of June, 1816. On the
9th of August the foundation stone of the Bath Road School Room
was laid, and on the 6th of January the school took possession;
the number of scholars at the time consisting of 184 boys and 148
girls.

1817—Long Room added to the Montpellier.

Previous to the erection of the Long Room here referred to, the
Pump Room of the Montpellier consisted merely of a large square
building, with a wooden veranda in front.

1817—June 11, Sherborne Promenade began.

1818—February, Roman Baths discovered at Witcomb.

1818—September 28, Town first lighted with gas.

1818—October, Savings' Bank established.

1818—August 12, Sherborne Spa opened.

> The establishment of the Sherborne Spa tended greatly to the improvement of Cheltenham, by converting a large tract of marshy ground into beautiful rides and drives. The Promenade forming the present approach to the Montpellier property was laid out and planted, and a bridge erected over the Chelt in June 1817. The first stone of the Pump Room was laid January 19, 1818. It changed its name some years after from the *Sherborne* to the *Imperial*. But this room itself has now ceased to exist, at least in connection with a Spa, having been taken down to make way for the present Queen's Hotel on its scite. The Room has, however, been re-erected at the end of the Imperial Promenade, immediately over the Chelt, and adds greatly to the architectural appearance of that part of the town.

1818—April 25, Chelt overflowed, great damage.

> The flood here spoken of overflowed the lands on both sides of the river to an alarming extent, and did very great damage. The Sandford meadows were laid under water.

1819—Cheltenham races established.

> In the August of the previous year experimental races were held on Nottingham Hill; their success led to the establishment of those which have annually taken place on Cleeve Hill, and which are the races here referred to.

1819—Spring at the Old Well deepened to 70 feet.

1819—April 6, Gas Light Act obtained.

1820—January 22, A. Fothringham, Esq., M.C., died.

1820—March 21, Charles H. Marshall, Esq., elected M.C.

> Capt. Marshall succeeded Mr. Fothringham, who died January 22nd of this year.

1820—November 2, H. Thompson, Esq., died, aged 72.

> To Henry Thompson, Esq., the Town of Cheltenham stands more indebted for its present "high and palmy state" than to any other person, living or dead. The discoveries which he made in connection with its mineral waters, and the extensive improvements which he projected and accomplished on the Montpellier Property,

gave a reputation and celebrity to the place which, down to the period of his enterprising speculations, it had never enjoyed. His memory is still fondly cherished in the recollection of the inhabitants, as the town's benefactor; for, to use the forcible expression of the London Magazine of that day, " he left a name behind him of which no man could speak evil."

1821—Baptist Chapel re-built.

1821—June 29, first Van from Cheltenham to London.

Prior to 1831 there was no conveyance for heavy goods to London, except the broad-wheel waggons, which were usually four days on the road.

1821—June 23, Town Commissioners' Act passed.

This Act, which repealed two former Acts of Parliament, passed in the 26th and 46th of George the Third, for improving, cleansing, and lighting the town, granted enlarged powers for those purposes to the Commissioners appointed by and under this Act, who now have cognizance of all matters connected with the paving, lighting, and improving the town.

1821—Population, according to census, 13,388. Inhabited Houses 2411.

1821—Sept. 14, George the Fourth passed through Cheltenham on his return from Ireland.

1821—Dec. 5, Thomas Bagott De la Bere, Esq., died, aged 93.

Thomas Bagott de la Bere was the only surviving representative of a very ancient family who had come over with William the Conqueror, and who for many generations had lived at Southam, considered one of the oldest residencies in Gloucestershire. The " last of his race," Thomas Bagott de la Bere was always known as " the Squire," by which appellation he was generally addressed, and his health drank at public dinners. Upon his death the estate was purchased by Lord Ellenborough, who made it his place of usual residence.

1822—May 22, Bath Road, through Painswick, opened.

1822—July 30—Mr. Griffith ascended with Green in his balloon.

This was the first balloon inflated in Cheltenham with the common gas.

1822—August 5, New Market opened.

Previous to the erection of the present commodious building the Market House stood near the centre of the High Street, on the scite of the Public Office. The new Market House and Arcade were built at the expense of Lord Sherborne, the then Lord of the Manor, who received the income arising from the tolls and rent-charges.

1822—July 10, visit of the Prince and Princess of Denmark.

1823—January 26, Dr. Jenner died, aged 74.

This eminent benefactor of the human race was long and intimately connected with Cheltenham, having practised here as a physician for many years. He was buried in the Parish Church of Berkeley on Monday, February the 3rd, 1828. On the 19th of August a masonic procession took place at Gloucester to assist at the erection of the monument to his memory.

1823—April 11, Trinity Church consecrated by Dr. Bethell, Bishop of Gloucester.

This church is mostly the property of the Lord of the Manor, Lord Sherborne having, on the failure of the subscriptions entered into for its erection, completed the edifice at his own cost.

1823—May 20, Parish boundaries perambulated.

Remarkable from the circumstance of there having been no previous perambulation for nearly a century. It occupied two days, and the ground gone over exceeded 26 miles.

1823—September 8, Foundation stone of the Mythe Bridge laid with Masonic honours.

The Mythe Bridge is erected over the Severn at Tewkesbury, and was considered of such importance to Cheltenham as opening the communication with Hereford, that a public procession was undertaken to lay the foundation stone.

1823—September 24, Mr. Graham ascended in his Balloon.

1323—November 5, First Lodge held in the Masonic Hall.

In the Masonic Hall, which was opened on the above occasion two Lodges are held,—the Foundation Lodge, removed from Abingdon, and the Royal Union from Cirencester.

1824—April 26, Eight new bells erected in the Parish Church.

This set of bells, erected at the expense of the parish, being incomplete, the ringers, at their own cost, added two others to perfect the peal: there are, therefore, at present ten bells.

1824—June 17, Water Works Company established.

1824—August 4, Dr. Jameson died, aged 71.

Dr. Jameson was one of the first physicians of his day in Cheltenham. He interested himself greatly in the discoveries of the late Henry Thompson, Esq., and wrote a Treatise on the Chemical and Medical Properties of the Cheltenham Waters, still referred to as the text book of their history.

1824—November 8, Cheltenham Journal first published.

1825—May 4, Foundation Stone of Pittville Pump Room laid with Masonic honours.

1825—June 1, First Mechanics' Institution formed.

1825—July 21, Montpellier Promenades first lighted with gas.

1825—August 4, Trial of Judge v. Berkeley.

1825—Nov. 29, Foundation Stone of St. James's Church laid.

1826—Alstone Infants' School (Wilderspin's) established.

1826—Montpellier Rotunda opened.

1826—August 24, First Ball at the Rotunda.

1826—September 28, Rev. Charles Jervis died.

1826—Nov. 19, Rev. F. Close inducted as Incumbent of Cheltenham.

1826—November 22, Sir W. Scott's visit.

1827—July 31, Duchess of Clarence's visit.

1828—Cheltenham Infants' School established in St. James's Sq.

The building, now the School Room, was not opened until the 26th of July, 1830.

1828—January 13, Parish Church lighted with gas.

1828—February 21, Public Clock set up.

1829—January 22, St. John's Church consecrated.

St. John's Church was built at the joint expense of the Rev. Spencer Phillips and the Rev. Mr. Moxon; the latter gentleman, however, died before the consecration took place.

1829—October 11, Dr. Christie, M.D., died suddenly.

Dr. C. was long a resident physician, and took an active part in the establishment of the Dispensary.

R

1830—June 10, Cobbett's visit.

This visit of the above celebrated political writer was very short; for having, unfortunately, in one of the early numbers of his famous Register, written a violent and coarse attack upon Cheltenham, the announcement which he made of an intention to deliver a political lecture in the Market Place, so roused the indignation of the inhabitants, that Mr. Cobbett found it advisable to decamp privately and in haste, and the day following his arrival he took his departure for Stow-on-the-Wold. The populace, disappointed of the opportunity of retaliating, burnt him in effigy through the streets.

1830—July 20, Pittville Pump Room opened, with a public breakfast.

1830—July 28, Montpellier Gardens opened.

1830—August 14, Visit of the Duchess of Kent and Princess Victoria.

1830—October 5, St. James's Church consecrated by Dr. Monk, Bishop of Gloucester.

St. James's Church was built in shares, mostly of one hundred pounds each: when completed the shareholders drew lots for the priority of selection, four hundred sittings having been first set apart for the endowment of the church. It is capable of accommodating about fourteen hundred persons.

1830—December 4, Mounted Association formed.

1831—Population according to census, 22,942; Inhabited houses, 4018.

1831—September 10, Col. Berkeley created Lord Segrave.

1831—Feb. 15, Gurney's Steam Coach exhibited in the streets.

This was the first and only attempt made in Cheltenham to run steam carriages on the public roads. Sir Charles Dance, who conducted this experiment, after exhibiting the carriage around the Montpellier and other public drives, for a few days, started it as a regular stage coach, to and from Gloucester. For some weeks it succeeded remarkably well, but on the roads being repaired, and fresh stone laid down, it was obliged to be abandoned.

1831—March 1, Cambrian Festival established.

1831—March 22, Opening Performance for the Organ at St. James's Church.

1831—May 9, Parish boundaries perambulated a second time.

1831—June 6, *L'Hirondelle* Coach started.

> *L'Hirondelle* was the first coach started, to run between Cheltenham and Liverpool daily, and performing the entire journey in one day.

1831—June 19, Races removed to Prestbury Park.

1831—July 12, St. Paul's Church consecrated.

1831—August 25, Visit of the Grand Duchesse Helene of Russia.

1831—Sept. 19, New Burial Ground opened.

1831—Sept. 26, Great Reform Dinner at the Assembly Rooms.

1831—Nov. 4, Police established.

> Previously to the establishment of the Police the old system of Watch prevailed. This Constabulary force was subject to the jurisdiction of the Town Commissioners.

1832—Feb. 3, Dr. Bell died at Lindsey Cottage, aged 80.

> Dr. Bell had been a resident of Cheltenham for several years before his death. Lindsey Cottage, the house in which he lived, is now occupied by Sir Richard Wolseley, and is called Wolseley Cottage.

1832—February 10, Dr. Bell buried at Westminster Abbey.

1832—March 21, Fast Day on account of the Cholera.

1832—Board of Health established.

> The escape of Cheltenham from the Cholera was probably to be attributed, in a great measure, to the establishment of the Board of Health. The exertions made by its members, to prevent and guard against the introduction of the infection and disease, are entitled to every possible praise. All the low and unhealthy places in the town were, under their superintendence and direction, thoroughly cleansed and purified; and the utmost care taken to prevent the spread of those fevers too commonly prevalent in a state of incipiency among the dwellings of the wretched and the poor. As an instance of the vigilance of this Board it may be mentioned, that in the autumn of 1832 nearly 2000 vagrants were prevented entering the town, being conveyed by its officers around the outskirts, relieved, and passed on their journey.

1832—Aug. 10, Reform Illumination.

1832—Nov. 14, Thanksgiving day for escape from Cholera.

1832—Dec. 10, Hon. C. F. Berkeley elected first Member of Parliament for Cheltenham.

1832—Montpellier Avenue opened.

1833—Jan. 23, Meeting to form Literary Institution.

1833—April 20, Cheltenham Sewerage Act obtained.

1833—May 4, Cheltenham Looker-On first published.

1833—July 9, Gloucestershire Chronicle first published.

1833—Oct. 22, First Conversazione at the Literary and Philosophical Institution.

1834—March 3, Mechanics' Institution formed.

1834—October, Cambray Chalybeate Spa opened.

1834—Oct. 23, Sir William Hicks died, aged 82.

Sir W. Hicks was for many years the only acting magistrate in Cheltenham.

1834—Nov. 1, Cheltenham Free Press first published.

1835—Jan. 8, Election. The Hon. C. F. Berkeley elected a second time M.P. for Cheltenham.

The Hon. Craven Berkeley was opposed on this occasion by W. P. Gaskell, Esq., but returned by a majority of 387 votes, only 25 having been polled for Mr. Gaskell.

1835—Jan. 10, C. W. Codrington, Esq., and the Hon. A. Moreton, elected Members of Parliament for the Eastern Division of Gloucestershire.

1835—April 6, The Cheltenham Athenæum opened.

The Athenæum was a literary and philosophical society, the rooms of which were in Portland Street. It orginally sprang from a schism which arose among the members of the Mechanic's Institution respecting the admission into that Society of political and religious questions, of which the founders of the Athenæum disapproved. It embraced the same objects as most similar societies, but for want of adequate support the society has now ceased to exist.

1835—April 26, Capt Grey died, aged 63.

Capt. Grey was for twenty years a resident of Cheltenham, during the whole of which period he took a most active part in almost every measure connected with the town, whether parochial or political. He commanded the first troop of Gloucestershire Yeomanry raised during the French War, and had a handsome piece of plate presented to him by the Officers, August the 15th, 1809. His remains were honoured with a public funeral, and interred in St. Mary's Churchyard on the 2nd of May, 1835. Earl Fitzhardinge and John Browne, Esq., of Salperton, were among the pall-bearers.

1835—June 8, Capt. Kirwan elected M.C.

Capt. Kirwan succeeded Mr. Marshall in the office. On Mr. Marshall's resignation several gentlemen announced themselves as candidates for the situation; but only one, Mr. Sisson, came forward on the day of election. Capt. Kirwan was returned by a majority of 235 votes.

1835—July 14, Races removed back to Cleeve Hill.

1835—Sept. 8, Triennial Visitation of Dr. Monk, Bishop of Gloucester.

No Visitation had taken place previously to this for thirty-four years, the Bishop of Gloucester having transferred that honour to Tewkesbury. On Dr. Monk's restoring it to Cheltenham on this occasion, a deputation of the inhabitants waited upon his Lordship to thank him for this mark of ecclesiastical favour, and afterwards, at his invitation, dined with him at Yearsley's Hotel.

1835—Nov. 10, First Meeting of the Board of Guardians.

1835—Dec. 8, Earl Fitzhardinge appointed Lord Lieutenant of the County.

1836—Feb. 28, Mr. John Gardner died, aged 70.

1836—March 25, Board of Highways instituted.

1836—Aug. 30, New Rooms of Literary and Philosophical Institution opened by Public Meetings.

1836—Oct. 19, Bishop of Gloucester formally took possession of the See of Bristol.

1837—July 3, Ascent of the Royal Vauxhall Nassau Balloon from the Montpellier Gardens.

This was the first ascent of this famous aeronautical machine out of the Metropolis. The inflation of the balloon occupied from midnight of the second till five o'clock in the afternoon of the third, at which hour Mr. Green, accompanied by Mr. Hughes, (one of the proprietors of Vauxhall) Mr. Spinney, (the Manager of the Cheltenham Gas Works) Mr. R. Jearrad, Mr. S. Moss, Chemist, and another individual, entered the car and ascended in beautiful style, in the presence of the assembled thousands who were in and around the Gardens. The party, after a voyage of one hour and twenty-five minutes, alighted at Ashton Keyms, near Cirencester. A full and minute account of the ascent and voyage appeared at the time in No. 84 of the *Cheltenham Looker On.*

1837—July 23, Hon. C. F. Berkeley elected third time member of Parliament for Cheltenham.

He was opposed by Jonathan Peel, Esq., on the Conservative interest, but returned by a majority of 334 votes.

1837.—October 10, Foundation Stone of Christ Church, Alstone, laid by the Rev. F. Close.

1838—April 23, Foundation Stone of St. Philip's Church laid.

1838—August 8, Grand Fête at the Royal Old Wells, to celebrate the Centenary of the establishment of the Spas.

1838—October 3, Mr. Hampton accomplished a successful descent in his safety Parachute from the Albion Balloon, which ascended from the Montpellier Gardens, being at the moment of separating the Parachute about two miles from the earth.

1839—May. The Cheltenham Theatre destroyed by fire.

1840—Jan. 26, Christ Church, Lansdown, consecrated.

1840—May 1, St. Philip's Church, Leckhampton, consecrated.

1841—Census taken. Population of the Parish of Cheltenham 31,385; or, including the Parishes comprehended in the Poor Law Union, 40,215.

1841—May 31, Opening of the Cheltenham and Great Western Union Railway, from Swindon to Cirencester.

1841—July 29, Proprietary College commenced.

1843—March 16, Manor of Cheltenham purchased from Lord Sherborne, by Mrs. Gardner and James Agg Gardner, Esq.

The Manor of Cheltenham, which the ancestor of Lord Sherborne bought in 1628 for £1,200, was now sold, with other properties in the Borough, for £39,000.

1843—May 12, the first Court Leet and Court Baron of the new Lady and Lord of the Manor held.

No. II.

MEASUREMENT OF SOME OF THE PRINCIPAL STREETS IN CHELTENHAM.

	YARDS.
From the Centre Stone to the London Gate	1693
" " to Tewkesbury Gate	2261
" " along Hewlett Street to Hewlett's Gate	2295
" " along Winchcomb Street to Prestbury Gate	1268
" " along Pittville Street to Evesham Gate	2102
" " along the Colonnade to Gloucester Gate	2738
" " along St. George's Place to Shurdington Gate	2602
" " along Bath Road to Leckhampton Gate	3216
" " to Hewlett Street	826
" " to Winchcomb Street	280
" " to Pittville Street	180
" " to Henrietta Street	160
" " to Coltham Lane	1306
" " to Cambray Place	406
" " to Tavistock Place	348
" " to the Colonnade	118
" " to St. George's Place	140
" " to Clarence Street	90
" " to St. George's Square	250
From High Street by Jersey Place to Hewlett's Gate	1469
" along Winchcomb Street to Prestbury Gate	988
" " Portland Street to Evesham Gate	1922
" " Henrietta Street to St. Paul's Church	635
" " Cambray to Leckhampton Gate	2810
" " Rodney Terrace to Montpellier Rotunda	1257
" " the Colonnade to St. James's Church	1335
" " the Colonnade to Gloucester Gate	2620
" " St. George's Place to the Park	1984
" " Clarence Street to the King's Well	693
" " New Street to the Albion Brewery	768
From the Tewkesbury Gate to the London Gate	3954

No. III.

LEVELS OF CHELTENHAM AND ITS VICINITY.

		FEET.
Base of Gloucester Cathedral, above Sharpness Point		60
Base of St. Mary's Church, Cheltenham	ditto	195
Summit of Bays Hill	ditto	239
Base of Charlton Church	ditto	292
Stratton Gate (Cirencester)	ditto	380
Waterworks Reservoir at Battledown	ditto	435
Churchdown Hill	ditto	500
Springhead of the Cheltenham Water-Works	ditto	672
Beeches Pike	ditto	820
Stow-on-the-Wold	ditto	883
High Cross, near Elkstone	ditto	878
Leckhampton Hill	ditto	925
Cleeve Cloud Hill	ditto	1134
Malvern Hill	ditto	1444

Height of St. Mary's Steeple .... 167 ft. 3 in.

No. IV.

LEVELS OF CHELTENHAM ABOVE THE BED OF THE RIVER AT LOWER ALSTONE MILL, CALCULATED BY MR. S. H. MERRETT.

	FEET.	
The Rail Road—Albion Brewery	24	41
Gloucester Turnpike	26	79
Cambray Spa	40	33
Yearsley's Hotel	41	23
Arcade	43	25
Montpellier Baths	44	—
Colonnade	45	26
Royal Wells	46	41
Plough Hotel	48	45
Imperial Spa	52	03
Pittville Pump Room	63	5
Montpellier Rotunda	73	33
Thirlestane House	83	26
Bays Hill Lodge	87	26

INDEX.

H. DAVIES, MONTPELLIER LIBRARY, CHELTENHAM.

CPSIA information can be obtained at www.ICGtesting.com
Printed in the USA
BVOW06s1244130214

344843BV00010B/272/P